The FINANCIAL PROFESSIONAL'S StoryBook

SCOTT WEST, DAVID SAYLOR & MITCH ANTHONY

ILLUSTRATIONS BY GREG WIMMER

Managing Editor: Debbie Anthony
Project Editors: Suzanne Norby, MD, Catherine Armstrong
Interior Design: Greg Wimmer
Illustrations: Greg Wimmer
Cover Design: Mark Lie, Aaron Krueger

Published by Advisor Insights Press

ISBN: 0-9727523-1-5

Preface vi

Chapter 1 – Value of a Good Advisor
Driving on Toll Roads 2
St. Andrews 3
On the Football Field 4
Security Systems 5
Tandem Skydiving 6
Navigator 7
Professional Guide 8
Piloting a Plane 9
Your Job—My Job 10
Vegetable Gardens 11
Caddies 12
Ten Reasons to Invest in No-Load Funds 13
Exclusive Vacations 14
Pilots 15
Knockout Roses 16
Bridge Over Troubled Waters 17
The CFP Soccer Coach 18
Finding an Advisor You Trust 19
The Need for an Advisor Who Pays Attention .. 20
Cruising Fast on an Empty Tank 21
Knowing the Ropes 22
Flying Alone 23
Do-It-Yourself Investing 24
The Financial Travel Agent 25

Chapter 2 – Need for Financial Planning
Catering 28
Travel Agent 29
Duck Hunting 30
Military Plans 31
The Missing Ingredient 32
Cross-Country Racing 33
Sailing 34
Flight Plan 35
The Game of Life 36
Visualizing the Space 37

Chapter 3 – Risk Management
Safety Chutes 40
Lifting Weights 41
Like Fine Wine 42
Guaranteed Fun 43
Like Riding a Bike 44
Fly Fishing 45
GMIB Cartoon 46
Playing with House Money 47
Green—Blue—Black 48
Life Insurance/Annuities 49

Chapter 4 – Equity Investing
Mouse Traps 52
Real Estate 53
Investing in Chickens 54
Your First Car 55
Sherman Tanks 56
Apple Trees 57
Sales 58
Growth Spurts 59
"Riding" the Right Investment 60
Farmer's Market 61
Lifeguards 62
Jack La Lanne's Fitness Approach 63
Injured Reserve 64
Stick Your Toe In 65
Monopoly 66
The Tale of the Genie and the Bottle 67
A-B-C Shares 68

Chapter 5 – Assorted Investment Strategies
Part One: Fixed Income Investing
Choosing Tenants 70
From Roller Coasters to Escalators 71
Teeter-Totters 72
Just in Case 73
Growing Fruit Trees 74

Part Two: Global Investing
Guests. 75
Michelle 76
Part Three: Unit Investment Trusts
Bottled Water 77
Perennials and Annuals 78
The Staple Remover. 79
Pictures and Videos 80
Car Leases 81

Chapter 6 – Asset Allocation/ Diversification

Window Panes 84
Farming 85
Rodeo. 86
Life Savers 87
Four-Wheel Drive 88
Three Little Pigs. 89
Basketball Teams 90
One-Club Golfers. 91
Body Builder 92
Gretzky. 93
Ferris Wheel. 94
The Financial Pyramid. 95
Soccer Positions. 96
Shoes in the Closet. 97
Building a Portfolio with Diversified Vehicles . . 98
Your Retirement Plane 99
Packing for All Climates 100
One Headlight 101
Confidence in Your Vessel 102
All-Star Game 103
Blending Colors 104
Ping-Pong Shots. 105
Tools for Building 106
The Portfolio Draft. 107
Breaking Pencils. 108
Elevator Cables 109
Ice Skating 110
"Wealthopoly" 111
Longwood Gardens 112
Picture Windows 113

Growth in the Garden. 114
The Tool Belt 115
Guitar Strings 116

Chapter 7 – Protecting Investments/ Taxation

Russian Doll Set. 118
Frequent Flyer Miles 119
Cheap Sneakers 120
The Fox and the Henhouse 121
Duty-Free Store 122
The "AnnuiTree" 123
The Kitchen Conversation 124
Lane Bumpers 125
Guardrails 126
Modern Auto Safety. 127
The Reset Button 128
Digital Camera Warranty 129
Swimsuit. 130
Roller Coaster. 131
Guaranteed Par. 132
Pitons 133
Uncle Sam and the Angel Food Cake 134
Leaks 135
Aerodynamic Tax Returns 136
Marathons 137
Racing Performance. 138
Ski Tuning 139
Shark Cage. 140
Lump-Sum Rollover. 141

Chapter 8 – The Time to Invest

Easing into the Water. 144
Splitting from the Herd 145
The Only Check to Bounce 146
The Measuring Tape. 147
Paychecks. 148
Moving Into the Market. 149

Chapter 9 – Long-Term Perspectives

Steadfast Training. 152
Mark McGwire. 153

Getting out of Rough Seas 154
Facing the Bear 155
The Best Time to Jump in the Markets 156
Michael Jordan's Stats 157
Meaningful Measurements 158
The Brick 159
The Yo-Yo and the Hill 160
Waves and Tides 161
Sticking with a Winner 162
Livestock 163
The Power of a Pawn 164
Dollar Cost Averaging 165
Marathon Training 166

Chapter 10 – The Impact of Inflation

A Modern Tale About Rip Van Winkle 168
Football Salaries 169
Golfing Against the Wind 170
Walking Up the Down Escalator 171
A First-Class Stamp 172

Chapter 11 – Investment Basics

Mulching 174
Selecting Tires 175
Grocery Shopping 176
Your Money and Your Life 177
College Courses and Degrees 178
Building a Pyramid for Your Assets 179
Gambling Versus Investing 180
Microwave Popcorn 181
Perennials 182
Winter Crops 183
How the Market Prices Stocks 184
There Goes the Neighborhood 185

Chapter 12 – Investment Wisdom

Dead Reckoning 188
Eluding the Bears 189
Remote Controls 190
Bad Nutrition 191
Hot Air Ballooning 192
Planting a Seed 193

Burnt Apple Pie 194
Investments for Life 195
Batting Singles and Doubles 196
Financial Fitness 197
Confidence in Your Vessel 198
Famous Names 199
"Seasonality" of Investing 200
Running Pace 201
Traffic Jam 202
The Right Reaction 203
The Right Response 204
Rear-View Mirror 205
Titanic 206
The "Retirement Green Jacket" 207
Edison 208
Roller Coasters 209
A Reliable Vehicle 210
Law of Lift 211
Chasing Losses 212
Bugs in the Light 213
Money Ball 214
Hang Ten 215
Coming Up Roses 216
Give It Your Best Shot 217
Waterlogged? 218
Butter or Margarine? 219
Portage in Rough Waters 220
The HALT Rule 221
Chasing the Hot Fund 222
Stock Value Versus Yield 223

We'd like to tell you a story...about *StorySelling*.

Little did we know when we published *StorySelling for Financial Advisors* (Dearborn 2000) the nerve it would strike in the industry. Since its release, *StorySelling for Financial Advisors* has become one of the all-time best-selling books for financial advisors. One in eight financial advisors in America has purchased the book, one in four has listened to a live presentation on the topic, and hundreds more have attended half-day or full-day seminars to learn how to develop stories to fit their businesses.

Maybe it was the timing of the market swoon and the resulting focus on building better client relationships. Or maybe it was the novel, fresh approach using analogies, metaphors, and illustrations to explain difficult investment concepts. We suspect that it is something more than that. The "something more" is that the *StorySelling* approach just feels right to both advisor and client. This approach is a better way to communicate, resulting in better client connections, which in turn, create a better business. In a marketplace where consumers are confused about what to do with their financial lives and about with whom to do business, the *StorySelling* approach brings needed clarity and calm to the advisor-client relationship.

Two great developments have evolved since the publication of the original *StorySelling* book. First of all, many advisors have either submitted their favorite stories to our websites (www.mitchanthony.com and www.vankampen.com), or have personally shared their stories with us after our speeches. You will see many of their stories in this volume. For example, one advisor from Baltimore shared a brilliant analogy on how to talk to clients about the value of advice. You'll find that story on page 17. Another advisor from Atlanta shared a great story about choosing the right bond. You'll find that story on page 70.

The majority of these stories have come from the second great development: our "Telling the Financial Story" seminar. During this seminar, advisors learn how to develop stories for themselves and their firms. For the last three years, we have had the opportunity to assist large institutions as well as individual advisors to hone the craft of developing metaphors, analogies, and illustrations that bring clarity to their products and services. As a result, both individual advisors and wholesalers have learned to differentiate their personal stories from the information overload that is all too common in a crowded and often confusing marketplace.

In these seminars, we teach advisors how to build a bridge between that which is known to the client (a hobby, an element of their life), and something which is unknown (an investment product, service, or concept). That bridge is commonly known as a metaphor. It's exciting to see the lights turn on in the clients' eyes and observe their willingness to act when advisors speak their own language, instead of financial-industry jargon.

One advisor shared his struggle to help clients understand why index funds were probably the worst investment they could make during this market period. He was trying to demonstrate the value of a good money manager in a fluctuating market cycle. Despite trying his best using numbers logic, he saw very little results. After going through the training and learning to change his strategy from "telling a story of numbers" to "telling a number of stories," he discovered that the key to explaining this money manager strategy was in his favorite hobby—boating. Here's the story we helped him develop:

"The market cycle we are in reminds me of my favorite hobby—boating. When the wind is blowing and you know the direction it is blowing, all you have to do is put up a sail, and the wind will take you where you want to go. That's what it is like in a bull market, such as we had in the late 90s. Index funds are like a sailboat. If the winds of the bull market are blowing, you can put up your sail (index funds) and do just fine. But if there is no wind—like the market we are in now—then your best chance to make progress in the water is to use your oars and paddle. It takes human effort and diligence to make progress without a wind. That's what money managers do—they use their oars and paddle to actively look for opportunities to move their clients' boats toward their destination."

Once he started sharing this analogy with his clients, they began understanding the difference and were willing to act on their own behalf. People understand the world around them much better than they understand the financial world. That is why *StorySelling* strategies work so well—they frame your story in the language of the client.

A key individual in gathering and refining stories, and in helping firms and advisors develop stories has been Dave Saylor, a campaign consultant at VanKampen Consulting. His work has been so outstanding that we asked him to join us as an author in this sequel. Another great benefit you'll find in this book is the imaginative illustrative work of Gregory Wimmer, whose artistry succeeds in bringing these stories to life.

In this book, we offer 200 more illustrations, analogies, and metaphors on topics ranging from the value of a good advisor, to asset allocation, to equities and annuities. Some stories were given to us by advisors such as Robyn Lewis (who made many contributions), while others have been seed ideas that flowered through editorial labor. Not only will these stories help make your client meetings more productive, they will also make them more fun. Happy reading.

– Scott West and Mitch Anthony

CHAPTER 1

VALUE OF A GOOD ADVISOR

Driving on Toll Roads

"The media often professes the benefits of self-directed investments. They argue that the fees hurt performance.

It's a little like arguing against toll roads. If you're taking a long trip, would you rather take the back roads or the toll roads? You can avoid the tolls by taking back roads; but in the end, the money you save on tolls will be consumed by the extra gas and mileage on your car. What's more, it's probably going to take you longer to reach your destination."

St. Andrews

"A few years back, I joined the local country club and started working on my game. I devoted some time to it, worked with a pro, and shaved 15–20 shots off my score. I was feeling pretty confident about my game—until I played the mighty St. Andrews Golf Course in Scotland.

St. Andrews is the oldest golf course in the world. The wind is brisk, the weather changes by the minute, there are 112 bunkers on the course, and the 17th green backs up to a road. The greens are so large that hundred-yard putts are common. St. Andrews quickly helped me discover the weaknesses in my game.

Unfortunately, it's a little like today's market, which has shown investors the weaknesses in their portfolios. It was too late by the time they discovered the problems. That's why you need an experienced professional on your side who already has played through the tough courses."

On the Football Field

"As a diehard football fan, would you suit up and play with the pros if given the opportunity? Would you step onto the turf with the big boys? I wouldn't. I don't need that kind of risk in my life.

It's a little like investing. When you make your own decisions, you're up against the professionals. The only difference is that there's no one to stop you from jumping into this game—and you can get hurt. That's why investors should use professionals."

Security Systems

"Most investors know what's happening in the business world. They read the papers, watch the news, and listen to the radio. They hear what the Fed is doing, what the Dow has done, and what the leading indicators are doing.

I think that's healthy, and I encourage it. But it's a little like having a home security system that isn't wired to the local law enforcement. If the alarms go off and there's no one standing by prepared to take action, then you're living with a false sense of security. One component of our service is to monitor what's happening and take the right actions when the alarms go off."

Tandem Skydiving

"Skydiving is not that difficult. With one morning of instruction, people can learn all they need to know about making a safe jump. Nonetheless, beginners are still required to jump with professionals. Do you know why? Because there's a big difference between knowledge and experience. Beginners have been known to panic. When something doesn't feel right, or something unexpected happens, they get frazzled and can actually put themselves in greater danger.

The same is true of investing. When the markets don't perform as planned, investors panic. In the 90s, they feared they weren't making as much as their neighbors, so they overweighted their portfolios in aggressive investments.. When the markets turned, they panicked and shifted all their money into conservative investments.

Both situations are dangerous for long-term investors. That's why investors—like skydivers—need the assistance of professionals."

Navigator

"Long-term investing is a little like a cross-country road trip. You're the driver, and I'm the navigator. I have all the maps and I know the route. I'm going to do my best to guide you along the most direct route with the fewest tolls—which are like taxes. I'm going to have the latest information on traffic congestion and road construction, and I'll make sure that you're driving at the appropriate speed at all times.

The bottom line is that I'm only here to help you make this journey—I can't make it for you. You will always be behind the wheel."

Professional Guide

"Let's say you're in the wilderness three hours from town and the sun is going down—and you have no idea where you are. Would you rather have a trail map or a guide?

It's a little like investing. You can go to the library or to the web and fumble through the financial trail maps, or you can choose a guide— a financial professional."

Piloting a Plane

"Good pilots have three basic skills:

- **Aviation**—how to fly.

- **Navigation**—how to get passengers to their destination.

- **Communication**—how to keep passengers informed of their progress.

The same is true of good investment professionals."

Your Job—My Job

Advisor to client: "You earn the seeds. I'll plant them."

Vegetable Gardens

"When clients ask one financial advisor why investors should pay fees and sales charges when they can invest online or in no-load funds for free, he asks them if they have ever tried to grow their own vegetables.

They usually respond that they have tried, but quickly add that they don't anymore because they just don't have the time to keep up with it.

Investing is a little like farming. Anyone can plant a seed, but only someone with the experience, the time, and the right tools can raise those seeds to their full potential. Remember, you rarely get a second chance to recover from a failed crop."

Caddies

"Some people don't like to pay financial advisors—and others do. I know of one guy who pays ten percent for advice, which is much higher than my fees. In fact, he reportedly paid his advisor $600,000 last year, even though he has access to magazines, books, and websites for a fraction of the price.[1]

Do you know who he is? Tiger Woods. His advisor and caddie is Steve Williams. Like other PGA Tour players, Tiger pays his caddie up to ten percent of his winnings for advice when he needs it."[2]

1 source: The New York Times (8/20/2000)

2 source: ESPN/Gold online ESPN.com (7/25/00) from Golf Week (5/15/00)

Ten Reasons to Invest in No-Load Funds

"Here are ten reasons to invest in no-load funds:

1. I feel secure in putting my hard-earned life savings in a mailbox and sending it to total strangers.

2. I prefer the service I receive from faceless clerks at 800 numbers to a local investment professional.

3. I have plenty of time to read financial journals, investment magazines, and newsletters.

4. I believe publications that depend on advertising revenue from no-load funds can render impartial and objective investment advice.

5. I prefer being thought of as a computer entry, rather than as a person.

6. I believe fund companies that sell to a mass market care about me and understand my specific financial goals, time horizons, and risk tolerance.

7. I have nerves of steel. The 507-point market decline on October 19, 1987, didn't concern me—nor do bear markets.

8. I can time the market and make fund switches with laser precision.

9. I don't find the 4,000+ no-load fund alternatives overwhelming. By reading five prospectuses a day, I'll know them all in about 26 months.

10. I am not willing to pay fees for professional services. In addition to managing my own investment portfolio, I also diagnose and treat my own medical problems, represent myself in legal matters, and file my own taxes."

(Van Kampen Funds)

Exclusive Vacations

"Let me ask you something. If you were planning a standard, no-frills family vacation to Disney World, would you need a travel agent? Probably not, because you could find a package deal on the internet.

What if you wanted to take your family somewhere that wasn't designed and built for the masses—a destination that was more interesting and a little less crowded? Do you think you would need a travel agent?

The same is true of investing. If you want the standard, no-frills investment in index funds or money markets, you don't really need the guidance of professionals. You'd be investing with the masses because that's who these investments are designed for.

But if you want a unique investment with potential for higher returns, you're going to need a 'travel agent' with local knowledge and years of experience."

Pilots

An advisor shared this illustration regarding style drift:

"I know from our previous visits that you like to travel, so let me ask you something. (He draws a map of the U.S. with three dots; one represents where they live, the second represents San Francisco, and the third represents San Diego.)

Suppose you boarded an airplane for San Francisco (he draws a line from the first dot halfway to the second dot), but the pilot instead decided to take you to San Diego (he changes the direction of the line to connect to the third dot). He felt that since the weather was nicer in San Diego, you and the other passengers would probably rather go there than San Francisco.

As unreasonable as this sounds, it's happening all the time with mutual funds. Mutual fund managers have discretion over what's in the fund—within certain legal limitations. Some change the direction of the portfolio without notifying the shareholders, and suddenly, the shareholders are taken to a different destination.

That's why I want you to invest in a fund with a long track record of style consistency. I like to keep my eye on the pilots to make sure they're not drifting off course."

Knockout Roses

"I promised my wife a rose garden—literally. I quickly realized this wasn't a good idea because I travel a lot. Roses need a great deal of nurturing and care, including drip irrigation, pruning, pesticides, mulch, and shelter from extreme temperatures. Nevertheless, a promise is a promise, and so I went to the store, paid for the roses, and planted them. As sometimes happens in gardening, I skipped a couple of steps (I didn't fertilize or prune) and paid the price—the roses died.

I then learned about a new breed of roses called knockout roses, which are genetically bred to be impervious to adverse climates and diseases. These roses lived up to the claims, and now my wife has her rose garden.

Well, I learned my lesson. It's a little like investing for retirement. People often buy, hold, and forget about their investments. Without systematized care, pruning, and nurturing, even the best plants can wither.

That is why we have an account program that automatically rebalances account portfolios each quarter. It ensures that we make the appropriate allocations to maintain your portfolio. If we aren't diligent about the care and protection of your portfolio, it's not going to grow."

Bridge Over Troubled Waters

An advisor in Baltimore, Maryland, shares this analogy with his mature clients:

"When you drive across the Annapolis Bridge, you have two choices. If you take the left-hand lanes, your toll is only $2.00, but there are no guardrails. If you choose the two right-hand lanes, it is going to cost you $2.50, but there is a guardrail. Which lanes would you prefer?

That's what I want to do for you. I want to be the guardrail—a safeguard for all your investment decisions."

The CFP Soccer Coach

"I'm a soccer coach for 11–12 year olds. I play many roles with them and have many responsibilities that are analogous to my role as a financial advisor. One of my chief responsibilities is to stay with these kids after practice until their parents pick them up. The rule is never to leave a player in the dark. I may have other things I need to do and other places I need to go, but I never violate this rule.

So it is in my role as an advisor. When events take place like we've seen in the last few years, I don't leave my clients alone in the dark. I have a responsibility to stay with them—by communicating and providing support. Advisors who follow this rule rarely—if ever—lose clients."

(Contributed by Gene Lawrence, CFP)

Finding an Advisor You Trust

An advisor in the Midwest once handed a kernel of corn to a farmer client and asked:

"Do you expect me to believe that you could somehow magically produce row upon row and acres upon acres of corn from this little kernel?

You and I both know you could. There is no questioning the potential of a seed. The real question would be, 'Do I believe in your competence as a farmer to get the job done? Am I willing to trust you with this seed?'

Your money is no different from this seed—it has the same potential. The only question you really need to answer is, 'Do you believe in my competence as an advisor to manage that growth?'"

The Need for an Advisor Who Pays Attention

"Have you ever planted a seed and forgotten to water it? If you have, there's more work to growing beautiful flowers than just dropping a seed in the ground. When the ground is dry, we water it. When it's cold, we protect it.

There are advisors who will show you a pretty picture of a flower, drop your investment seed in the ground, and then forget about it. Around here, we believe it's what we do after we plant the seed that matters."

Cruising Fast on an Empty Tank

An advisor who enjoys deep-sea fishing shared this nautical analogy:

"As we headed back to the bay, I remarked to the captain of the fishing boat about how much faster we seemed to be cruising on the way home compared to the ride out that morning.

The captain replied, 'You can go a whole lot faster when your tanks are almost empty. This morning our tanks were full, and it was a steady ride at a moderate speed. Now, closer to empty, we can really let it out.'

It made me think of good investment advice: when our tanks (brain power) are full, it's a steady and moderate ride; but when we push our clients for speed in important decisions, we might be riding on a nearly empty tank."

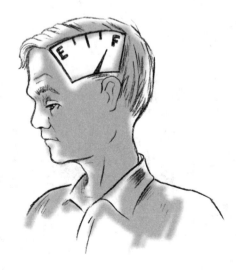

Knowing the Ropes

"Learning to direct a large sailing ship requires a great deal of learning. The newcomer to the sailing crew must memorize the functions of over a hundred hanging ropes that control the speed, direction, and stability of the ship. During a storm, if just one person on the crew lacks experience and pulls the wrong rope, it creates danger for everyone on board.

After what we have experienced in recent years, you want to make sure you have an advisor who knows the ropes."

Flying Alone

"What if you were going on a trip and you were offered the opportunity to fly on one of two jet airplanes? The first is piloted by an experienced pilot who is being paid to pilot. The second has no pilot, but you are allowed to fly the plane yourself. If you choose the plane without the pilot, the cockpit will contain a computer, which hooks you up to an internet site that will tell you everything you need to know about flying. Which plane do you want for your journey?

What you're paying for when you hire an advisor is not information—you can get that anywhere. You're paying for experience. I've been there in bad weather and know how to make a safe landing."

Do-It-Yourself Investing

"Do you really want to 'Home Deport' your portfolio? Here's what I mean. Instead of hiring a professional to repair that leaky faucet, you repair it yourself to save a few bucks. You make a few mistakes, the project gets more complicated than you thought, and you end up in the returns department because you bought parts for an fx-118, instead of an fx-119. In the end you've spent more money because you needed new tools, you've wasted a weekend, and you've got water damage behind the cabinets.

It's a little like do-it-yourself investing. If you make a mistake at investing, you might not know that this 'faucet' is leaking for months—or years—down the road. Then it's too late, and the market has a no-refund policy. You don't get your money back—not today, not tomorrow, and not at retirement. It's gone."

The Financial Travel Agent

"Think about this scenario. You want to go to Hawaii, but you don't specialize in travel, and so you call your travel agent. There are many ways to go to Hawaii. You can drive to California and take a boat; you can take a train to California, and then fly to Hawaii; or you can fly directly from your home. Your travel agent most likely will suggest you fly direct and will then pick the best airline for you.

Once you get to Hawaii, where will you stay? Your travel agent will ask if you want to stay in an inexpensive hotel, camp, or resort. Again, based on your wishes, your travel agent will find the best situation. How will you get around? Taxi? Rental car? What activities will you want to do? Snorkeling? Horseback riding? Hiking?

The bottom line is that you express your destination wishes to your travel agent, and your travel agent makes the trip happen. What if your airline goes on strike or your hotel burns down? Not to worry, your travel agent will make alternate arrangements.

A good financial advisor is simply your financial travel agent. You have a financial destination in mind ('I want to retire at age 65'; 'I want to be financially independent at age 60'; 'I want to send my grandchildren to college in ten years'), and you can convey that destination to your financial advisor.

Your advisor will examine all the vehicles that can get you to your destination and then choose those vehicles that will work best in your situation. If an obstacle arises (low interest rates, volatile market), your financial travel agent will find an alternate course. All you have to do is to focus on your financial destination and let your financial travel agent do the rest."

(Contributed by Robin Lewis)

CHAPTER 2

NEED FOR FINANCIAL PLANNING

Catering

"Every year my wife and I throw a big holiday party. At first, the parties were very manageable, and we could do everything. But over the years, they took on a life of their own. We spent so much time preparing guest lists, cooking food, answering the door, serving, and cleaning that we lost sight of the reason we were hosting these parties—to spend time with our family and friends. We weren't the hosts anymore, we were the kitchen help—and the parties suffered.

Last year, we decided to have the party catered, which freed us to host, entertain, and add some special touches like my homemade dessert. Not only did we enjoy the party more, our guests did, too.

Does this remind you of your portfolio? I know people who started their own investments with a hot tip or their company stock. As they grew older, they accumulated some money, opened more accounts, and bought some property. Over time, the investments demanded more of them than they demanded of their investments. They lost sight of the reasons they had invested in the first place, which was to enjoy their money. That's when they hired financial professionals—for the same reason we hired the caterer."

Travel Agent

"Let me tell you about a cruise I took with my wife. We left Boston in 28-degree weather and flew to Miami, where it was 85 degrees, sunny, and lovely—a great start.

Not long after we boarded the ship, we began to see clouds and more clouds, which turned into a hurricane. For seven straight days on the cruise, we did not see the sun. The boat rocked, tossed, and turned nonstop—and both of us became seasick. To add to the misery, our room, where we were spending all of our time, was next to the boiler room. It was a miserable experience and—not surprisingly—our last cruise.

It may sound like everything went wrong; but really, it all came down to one mistake—we didn't use our travel agent. If we had, she may have persuaded us not to go to the Caribbean during hurricane season. She may have sent us to Mexico, California, or even Florida. And she may have secured a better room than the one next to the boiler. We found out the hard way."

Duck Hunting

"If you want to be successful at duck hunting, you have to take advantage of your surroundings. For example, if the skies are clear, then you need to be well camouflaged and have your duck calls ready because you're going to have only a couple of opportunities to shoot ducks.

On the other hand, when the skies are dark, it's 25 degrees, and rain is pouring down, you don't have to worry about camouflage. You have to set up your positions so that everyone in your group can get opportunities in every direction. Since you can't see the ducks coming in from far away, you need to be prepared to get your shots off quickly. Because duck hunting is a very complex sport, novice hunters don't do very well.

It's a little like investing. You have to know how to take advantage of the different market conditions. That's why I encourage all my clients to develop a comprehensive investment plan."

Military Plans

"War historians often say that battles aren't won and lost in the field, they're won and lost in the planning.

It's the same with investing, which is why you need a comprehensive financial plan."

The Missing Ingredient

"This is a loaf of bread that didn't rise. The baker used the best ingredients (flour, salt, and eggs) to make the bread, but he overlooked one thing—the yeast. This is an example of how one missing ingredient can have a drastic impact on results.

That's why I encourage all of my clients to develop a comprehensive financial plan. A successful plan has many ingredients—investments, assets, liabilities, and debts. If you ignore any one of them, you could wind up with a financial situation that is a little . . . flat."

Cross-Country Racing

"Suppose someone challenges you to drive across the country in two days for a chance to win a prize of $1 million? What would your strategy be?

Let me offer some suggestions. First, you would get a map to chart the safest and most direct route to the West Coast. Second, you'd leave as soon as possible (the best way to arrive early is to start early). Third, you'd take a reliable vehicle with a track record of dependability.

That situation is a lot like investing for retirement. It's a long journey. You should start with a map (financial plan) to help you chart the safest and most direct route to your goal. Second, the earlier you invest, the earlier you arrive—in most cases. Third, you should take the most reliable and dependable vehicle you can."

Sailing

"I'd like to share a story with you about a sailing experience I had last summer. I went sailing with a few buddies of mine off the New Jersey shore. It was a beautiful summer day with a nice breeze. We were going along fine when, without warning, an enormous storm popped up. It happened so quickly that we got caught in the middle of it. Luckily, my buddies knew exactly what to do. They dropped the jib, reefed the mainsail, and switched tacks. It was automatic.

It was amazing watching them work together as a team. We were able to face the storm and get through it with no damage. Twenty minutes later, the storm passed, the sun came out, and the wind died. Fortunately, the boat was equipped with a motor so we were able to make it back to the marina. Although my buddies couldn't control the weather, they knew how to react to the changing conditions—and were prepared for everything.

Changing weather conditions are a little like the changing market conditions. Fund managers can't control the markets anymore than we can control the weather, but experienced fund managers know what to do in these financial storms."

Flight Plan

"Before I fly, there are three things I check every single time, because any one of them could spell disaster:

- **Myself**—Am I in a good enough condition to fly?
- **Weather**—Are the weather conditions safe for flying?
- **Plane** —Have I carefully double-checked every item on the checklist?

I believe these same rules apply to investors and investing:

- Are you in the right frame of mind and health for investing?
- Is the investment climate conducive?
- Has the investment vehicle been checked out thoroughly by someone with a trained eye?"

The Game of Life

One advisor keeps the board game "Life" on his desk when he meets with prospective clients.

"Do you see that game over there? That's how many financial advisors treat their relationships with clients. They set up the board and give them a great game strategy. But once they get the clients into their game, they hand the board back, leave them on their own, and look for another player.

I won't do that because I know that life isn't a game—you can't lose, close up the board, and simply play another day. Together we can determine a strategy, face any obstacles, and make it to the end successfully."

Visualizing the Space

"Good financial advisors are a lot like good interior decorators. They look at a room or a house and begin to visualize what it can become. They create a plan, pick out materials and furnishings, subcontract with providers who can deliver the quality their clients want, and see it through to completion. But it all begins with visualizing the space.

It's the same with your portfolio—how would you like your financial picture to look when it is done?"

CHAPTER 3

RISK MANAGEMENT

Safety Chutes

"I remember when I went skydiving for the first time. My girlfriend and I drove out to a little airstrip in Michigan and made the jump.

If you've ever done this, you find out very quickly that you have to sign about 30 legal documents before strapping on a chute. It made us a little nervous, and so my girlfriend turned to the instructor and asked, 'Has anyone ever died from this?'

'Yes,' he said. 'But, there's a 98 percent chance your chute will open.' Sensing our apprehension he added, 'For $10.00 you can rent an extra chute that would give you a 100 percent chance of the chute opening.'

So, I paid the extra $10.00 and went up in the plane. I made the tandem jump with the instructor strapped to my back. It was a great experience. We stepped out of the airplane into the open sky, flew backwards, did two flips for 35 seconds at 120 miles an hour, pulled the chute at 5,500 feet and it opened—no problem. We floated safely back to earth and I checked that off my to-do list.

It's a lot like investing—both are about managing risks. There are two key issues you need to consider with equity investing:

1. You need a professional with experience in managing risks.

2. You need a safety chute so that you don't lose everything."

Lifting Weights

"If you've ever lifted weights, you know that you shouldn't attempt to lift the maximum weight possible. Instead, you lift an amount you can manage and still keep your balance. Lifting too much weight can cause serious injuries.

So it is with risk tolerance. Don't bite off your maximum risk tolerance. Instead, adopt a balanced program—one that builds financial strength yet still allows you to sleep at night."

Like Fine Wine

"A good wine becomes more valuable with the passage of time.

That's the way we look at our clients. This particular annuity has a feature that rewards you for aging well—the older you get, the more we pay you."

Guaranteed Fun

"What if Donald Trump invited you to his casino and told you to gamble to your heart's content? And at the end of the night, if you won, you could keep the winnings. However, if you lost, he would restore your original amount. Would you do it?

That is exactly what this variable annuity allows you to do."

Like Riding a Bike

One advisor, an avid biker, likes to share this analogy.

"I have two types of bicycles at home—a mountain bike and a touring bike. If the terrain is rough or has lots of ups and downs, I use the mountain bike. If the terrain is fairly smooth, I use the touring bike for a smooth, consistent ride. In other words, I have different bikes for different terrains.

That's how I approach investing as well. This particular product gives you investment options to carry you through the level stretches as well as the ups and downs of the market."

Fly Fishing

"If you ever go fly fishing, there is one tip that can save your life (especially in a rapid current): don't go in water above your waders!

Once water fills your waders, you're in trouble. Take slow, steady, and vigilant steps to protect yourself. So it is with wading into unfamiliar investment terrains."

GMIB Cartoon

"As you know, a Guaranteed Minimum Income Benefit Rider (GMIB) allows individuals to invest in the market and, as a worst case scenario, provides a minimum guaranteed income stream based on either a hypothetical rate of return or a highest anniversary value.

Picture a roller coaster: people are screaming as it takes a big dive. The front of the roller coaster where the name of the ride usually is (The Beast, etc.) reads, 'Your Investment Account' or 'Your Mutual Funds,' etc. The caption on the cartoon reads, 'Not all roller coasters are fun.'"

(Contributed by Robin Lewis)

Playing with House Money

An advisor out East likes to share this analogy with his clients who occasionally visit the casinos in Atlantic City:

"Have you ever walked up to a table with $50, won a few hands, and, suddenly, found yourself up $400? When that happened, did you ever stick that original $50 stake back into your pocket and play the rest of the way with house money?

Which is easier to put at risk, your money or the house's money? Most would probably agree that it is easier to put the house's money at risk.

I like to have my clients look at how much money they have put up personally and how much money they have made from investment gains. I then suggest that they put the money they've put away in a safe place and use the house's money for the investments that have a higher degree of risk."

Green–Blue–Black

An advisor from Colorado shares this analogy:

"I wish I could put a colored diamond–green, blue, or black—on every prospectus I hand to clients. If they are skiers, they understand what I mean when I say that an investment is kind of like a blue hill (moderate skill required) or a black hill (expert skill required).

Before you enter a run in skiing, you have the comfort of knowing ahead of time the difficulty level you will face. That way, if your nerves are not up to the level and you want to relax, you can choose the green hill—which is safe even for the novice."

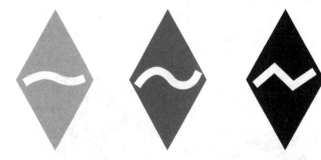

Life Insurance/Annuities

"I say transitioning from selling life insurance to selling annuities is a major paradigm change. Just look at what's going on with both products.

With life insurance, what are you betting happens? You are betting that you are going to die. With annuities, what are you betting on? You are betting that you are going to live.

With life insurance, what happens the older you get? The insurance company gets more money. With annuities, what happens the older you get? You get more money.

With life insurance, where are you when the policy does its grand finale? You are not in the audience to see it. With annuities, where are you when the policy does its grand finale? You are the star of the show!"

(Contributed by Robyn Lewis)

LIFE INSURANCE   **ANNUITIES**

CHAPTER 4

EQUITY INVESTING

Mouse Traps

"Do you recognize this (shows mouse trap)? It's the common 'snap trap' invented by John Mast back in 1899 to catch mice.

Over the years, many inventors have tried to come up with a better mouse-trap. There are over 4,400 registered patents on the mousetrap—with about 400 added each year. But the 'snap trap' is the one that most people still buy. Sometimes people just get it right the first time.

That's like value investing. Benjamin Graham, the Father of Investment Theory, proposed the benefits of buying stocks cheap back in 1934. Nearly 70 years later, it's still the most widely followed investment theory."

Real Estate

"I know from our previous meetings that you own some land. Of course, you hope that land will appreciate in value so that you can sell it for a higher price. Well, that's a lot like investing in growth stocks.

In the meantime, suppose you could lease the land to a farmer. He might grow some soybeans or corn on your property. The important part is that you'd earn some income from the property and still have growth potential.

That's like the concept behind dividends. You get growth potential from the appreciation of stocks, but you also have the potential for dividend income along the way."

Investing in Chickens

"Investing in equities is kind of like raising chickens. If the market for chickens goes up, you make a bigger profit on your investment. Would you ever invest in those chickens just for the growth potential? Of course not. You would invest with the expectation of selling the eggs.

That's a little like this growth and income fund. You capture the profit if the value of those stocks increase; moreover, since you're invested in stocks that have traditionally paid dividends, you have the potential to receive income as well."

Your First Car

"Do you remember your first car? Was it a brand-new Mercedes? Probably not. In fact, if it's anything like my first car, it was probably a 15-year-old clunker. I could sum up my first car experience this way: little money in, many miles out. It wasn't glamorous, but it was by far the best value I ever had in a car. Dollar for dollar, it got me farther than any other car I've owned .

That car reminds me of value investments. They are not the glamorous stocks that lead the news and make front pages of magazines; in fact, they're generally oversold and out-of-favor companies. That's why value managers snap them up—they're available at bargain prices. Dollar for dollar, they think that they can get more mileage out of that company than in glitzy growth stocks."

Sherman Tanks

"Growth and income funds can be a little like Sherman tanks for your portfolio. Just as Sherman tanks have armor for defense and cannons for offense, growth and income funds can hold fixed income for defense, and equities for offense—helping to prepare investors for more uncertainties ahead."

Apple Trees

"Growth and income funds are like the 'apple trees' of mutual funds. Not only do you have the potential for long-term growth, you also get to dine on some dividends along the way."

Sales

"Imagine that you are at the mall looking for a new book. There are two bookstores. One has a sign out front that reads, 'Sale—all prices reduced by 20–50 percent.' The other store has a sign out front that reads, 'All prices marked up an additional 20–50 percent.' Both stores have the book you're looking for, but the second store is much more crowded than the first. Which store will get your business?

Well, the market is always offering stocks that have been marked down by 20–50 percent. Are you going to wait for the markups?"

Growth Spurts

An advisor uses this with parents to illustrate growth stocks:

"How old are your children now? Did they ever go through a growth spurt—a time when they really shot up?

That's what the growth fund manager is looking for—stocks about to hit a growth spurt. They aren't interested in investing in a company when it's 6 feet 2 inches tall, they want to invest when it's still 5 feet 4 inches tall."

"Riding" the Right Investment

"Let me tell you a story about something we have in common—horseback riding. When I was a ten years old, my dad took my younger brother and me riding. I chose the horse I wanted to ride, and so my dad lifted me into the saddle. He put my brother on the other horse—a beautiful Shetland pony. My brother's pony took off as soon as he mounted. My brother started screaming and crying, so my dad quickly ran over and rescued him—leaving me alone on my horse. That's when my horse went crazy—he started bucking, and threw me off.

Fortunately, I was not seriously hurt, but the experience scared me to death. I never wanted to ride again. Two days later I learned that the horse I was riding wasn't really a horse—it was an ass.

Years later I met someone who loved horses, and so I told him about my experience. He told me that the key to riding is having a well-trained horse with a reputation for being steady and consistent (remember, behind every well-trained horse is a good trainer).

Your situation is very similar to mine—you were riding a very aggressive investment and had a bad experience. I'd like to put you on something with a track record of being steady and consistent—a fairly conservative growth and income fund. It's the best way to 'get back on the horse' in the equities market."

Farmer's Market

"I have a fantastic time-tested recipe for lasagna. The secret is in the ingredients. I go to the farmer's market and the butcher to hand-pick the best tomatoes, ripest peppers, and prime cuts of meats. I've learned through experience how to find the best ingredients that are not readily available in supermarkets. It makes my lasagna a crowd-pleaser and never lets anyone down.

This mutual fund is a little like my lasagna. The managers hand-pick investments—many of which are not available in the retail market. With this fund, you can participate in the institutional securities."

Lifeguards

"Do your children swim? My kids are at the city pool all the time. The only reason I let them go is because I have confidence in the lifeguards. They do not have just one lifeguard on duty, they have three—all experienced and certified. With so many kids in the water at the same time, they need a team of guards to spot trouble quickly and to pull the kids out before anyone gets hurt.

I feel the same way about mutual funds. If there are a hundred or more securities in a portfolio, they should have more than one portfolio manager on duty. The fund I'm about to show you is managed by a team who can spot potential problems and pull securities out of the portfolio more quickly than if they had just one manager. That is important to me, and it is one reason why I'm comfortable putting my clients into this fund."

Jack La Lanne's Fitness Approach

"Do you know anything about Jack La Lanne's exercise philosophy? It's not abdominal exercises, protein shakes, or diets that transform a person into Hercules over night. It's about all of these in a designed and disciplined combination over a long period of time.

La Lanne offers a regiment called the 'Magic 5,' which rotates stomach crunchers, leg curls, fanny firmers, running in place, and dynamic stretching. This philosophy has helped him stay in remarkable shape.

The managers we choose for equity and income funds have a similar approach to investing. They don't rely on just one or two investments to carry the performance of the fund. Instead, they use a disciplined mix of stocks, bonds, and preferreds for 'financial fitness.'"

Injured Reserve

"Many investors who were hurt in the bear market have become gun-shy about equities. This scenario reminds me of the way managers handle a professional baseball player who has been injured. They don't rush a pitcher back to the majors; they send him on rehab assignments to pitch in an inning or two in low-level minor league games, and then gradually increase the number of pitches and the level of competition. Managers do this to gradually restore the player's confidence and to test him slowly.

This is the same attitude we need to take toward re-entering the stock market—as if we're coming off the injured reserve."

Stick Your Toe In

"Re-entering the equities market is a lot like going into a pool. It takes a little time for our bodies to adjust to the temperature. There are some who like to dive in and take the initial shock—and get it over with. Most of us, however, prefer the 'toe-in' approach—we dip our toes in first, inch down the ladder, and then start wading in the shallow end.

That's the way to re-enter the equities markets since the waters have been somewhat cold lately."

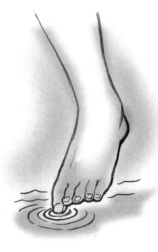

Monopoly

Try this with clients who question getting into the market right now.

"Have you ever played Monopoly? What happens when you circle the board? (Collect $200.) What does that $200 represent? (Wages.) Do you remember anyone who ever won the game by just circling the board and collecting their $200? Probably not. To win the game, you have to invest in properties and hotels so you can collect rent, etc.

Isn't the same true of our market? To win in the market, you have to invest in the market—and right now the prices are low. Enjoy the game!"

(Contributed by Robin Lewis)

The Tale of the Genie and the Bottle

"A man was walking along the beach one day. He was very distraught because he had recently lost his job, his bills were piling up, and he was afraid he might lose his home if something didn't change. As he was looking down, he saw a very strange-looking bottle. He bent over to pick up the bottle, and the top fell off. Suddenly, a genie appeared.

'You have freed me from my bottle,' he said. 'I will grant you one wish as my thanks.'

The man thought for a moment, 'If I win the lottery, all my trouble will be over.' He said to the genie, 'As my one wish, I would like to win the lottery.'

The genie smiled and said, 'Your wish is granted.'

The man was so excited that he took the bottle and ran all the way home. He waited all night for notification that he had won the lottery, but none came. He waited the next day, and the next, and the next—but still no lottery win. Days turned into weeks. Finally, the man grew very angry. He took the bottle and threw it against the wall.

Again the top fell off, and the genie appeared. 'Why are you so angry?'

'You said I would win the lottery, and I didn't. You lied—you did not grant my wish!' the man exclaimed.

'But I did grant your wish,' the genie said. 'However, you never bought a ticket!'

Clients wonder if they should invest in the market today. They wonder when the market will recover. There is no genie or crystal ball to tell us when that will occur. But history shows that after some of our nation's most infamous events, the market did eventually recover. The question is, 'Have you bought your ticket?'"

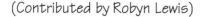

(Contributed by Robyn Lewis)

A-B-C Shares

Karen, a financial services sales trainer, shares this analogy to explain A, B, and C shares of mutual funds:

"When you go to McDonalds, you pay for your meal before you get your food. That's like an A share.

When you go to a finer restaurant, you sit down and eat and then pay for it. That's like a B share.

If you go to an all-inclusive resort, the cost of your meals is built into the total cost of your package. That's like a C share."

A   **B**   **C**

CHAPTER 5

ASSORTED INVESTMENT STRATEGIES

PART ONE—Fixed Income Strategies

Choosing Tenants

An advisor in Atlanta shares this analogy regarding bonds:

"With respect to credit risks, there are basically three types of bond funds:

- AAA Rated
- Investment-grade
- Below investment-grade.

Choosing between the three bond funds is a little like choosing tenants for your vacation property. You could rent to a mature couple for $700 a week, to a 30-something couple for $800 a week, or to college students for $1,000 a week. The potential profits increase with the potential risks."

$700 per week $800 per week $1,000 per week

PART ONE—Fixed Income Strategies

From Roller Coasters to Escalators

"Do you remember when you were young and loved to ride on roller coasters—when you actually liked the thrill of going up and down and getting tossed around?

Well, I've reached the age when I'd prefer an escalator to a roller coaster. I'd like to avoid the stress and stomach problems.

That's a little like this investment. It's not designed to give you the big ups and downs—just the potential for smaller and more stable gains."

PART ONE—Fixed Income Strategies

Teeter-Totters

"The relationship between fixed-income prices and interest rates is a little like teeter-totters. As interest rates rise, prices fall; as interest rates fall, prices rise.

Imagine that the stand for the teeter-totter is off-center—closer to the left. As yields rise and fall, prices rise and fall by less. That's kind of like short-term bonds.

Conversely, if the stand is closer to the other side, yields may rise and fall by a little, but prices will rise and fall by more. That's a little like long-term bonds."

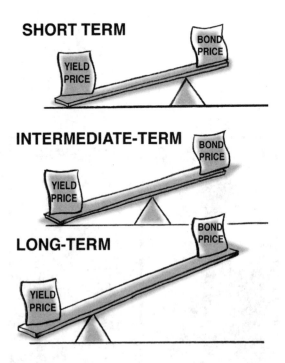

SHORT TERM

INTERMEDIATE-TERM

LONG-TERM

PART ONE—Fixed Income Strategies

Just in Case

"When clients ask why fixed income makes sense when stocks have outperformed bonds in the long-term, one advisor asks the following questions:

- Do you buckle your seat belt just to drive into town?

- Do you put a life raft on a perfectly sound boat?

- Do you have a fire extinguisher in your home even though there is no fire?

Maybe you should consider adding fixed-income investments to your portfolio—just in case."

PART ONE—Fixed Income Strategies

Growing Fruit Trees

"Let me tell you a story. When I was a young girl, my father taught me how to grow fruit trees. He showed me how to select the right soil quality, fertilizer, and location—with just the right amount of sunlight and water. He also showed me how to protect the trees from diseases and insects.

Although you have to work a little harder, a good fruit tree keeps bearing fruit. You can come back summer after summer and there will be more fruit. Best of all, you don't have to pay the grocer (or pay sales tax to Uncle Sam) because the fruit is yours.

It's a lot like finding a good municipal fund that has been around for a long time. It bears fruit every month that is yours to keep—it's tax exempt."

PART TWO—Global Investing

Guests

"There are two ways to travel in foreign countries—as tourists or as guests.

In 1993, we went to Paris as tourists. My college friends and I didn't speak French, and so we had a difficult time getting around and were treated poorly by the French. We stood in line at the Louvre, stood in crowds at Notre Dame, and walked everywhere because we weren't familiar with the public transportation system. Needless to say, it was a miserable experience.

The next time we traveled to France, we went as guests (a friend of my roommate lived there). She took us to all the right clubs, told us how to get museum tickets without waiting, and showed us how to get around the city without walking everywhere. It was an unbelievable experience: we ended up going back to Paris four times—as guests.

It's the same with global investing. You can invest either as a tourist or as a guest. If you invest globally through a fund in New York, or any other city in America, you may be investing as a tourist. Their fund managers may not have access to the best reports or have the local presence to know how to get things done and how to interview company management.

If you invest globally through an investment company with international presence, you're investing as a guest and will benefit from their local knowledge and global power."

Michelle

"Michelle is flying home on a Boeing 757. She's been in New York for nearly a week and needs to go to the store before going home. First, she stops at the GAP, and then she goes to the grocery store to pick up some Kleenex, Kellogg's Rice Krispies, Coke, GE light bulbs, Colgate toothpaste, and Pampers. When she walks in the door, her husband is sitting on the couch watching CNN with Madonna playing in the background.

What's unusual about that? Michelle lives in Paris, France.

The United States annually exports more than $20 billion worth of goods and services to France and over $780 billion to the world. You don't have to invest in foreign stocks to participate in global economies."

Bottled Water

"Unit investment trusts (UITs) are a little like bottled water. Bottled water is sold in clear containers so that consumers can see what they're getting—before they buy.

Unit trusts are sold the same way. Because UITs are fixed portfolios, investors can see the securities inside before they invest."

Perennials and Annuals

This is how one financial advisor explains the advantages of investing in both UITs and mutual funds:

"Do you know the difference between perennials and annuals? Perennials live indefinitely whereas annuals are seasonal. Landscapers recommend planting both, and here's why.

Over the long term, perennials can easily grow out of control. They can overtake the garden, the house, and even the lawn. You can get the same look—without losing control—by planting a combination of annuals and perennials.

That's a lot like mutual funds and UITs. Mutual funds are the perennials, and UITs are the annuals. The challenge with portfolio management is that mutual funds can have a hundred or more positions, and the portfolio manager can change them at any time. Multiply that times five or ten funds, and it gets pretty difficult to supervise. We have greater control of your portfolio when we have both mutual funds and UITs."

PART THREE—Unit Investment Trusts

The Staple Remover

One financial advisor explains the UIT concept by using a stapler, ream of paper, and staple remover.

"This ream of paper represents all of the stocks in the S&P 500. You can try to identify those that will perform well, or you can get help from one of the outstanding stock pickers of our time. (The financial advisor selects 10 to 50 sheets, staples them together, and hands the stapled sheets to the client.)

This stack represents a unit investment trust comprised of stocks selected by professionals. If the value of these stocks rise or fall, you keep the profits or the losses. You can hold on to the stocks and sell them back to us on any day the market is open, and you get the prevailing market price of that day. But if you redeem them too early, you may be subject to a redemption charge. You also have the option to hold them until the end of the term. Again, you get the prevailing market price at that time. That's what most people do. Or, you can take this staple remover and detach the certificates. (He detaches the sheets of paper.)

Now you own individual certificates, just as if you had bought them separately. You can sell some or all—or hold on to them, if you like. You are in control. In some cases, there can be tax advantages to doing this—ask your accountant.

That's how simple and straightforward UITs are. And, remember, they are the only ones to give you this—the staple remover."

PART THREE—Unit Investment Trusts

Pictures and Videos

"The differences between a UIT and mutual fund are similar to the differences between a camera and a video recorder.

One produces a picture that doesn't change—like a snapshot of your favorite scene. That's a UIT.

The other produces a film where the scenes do change. That's a mutual fund.

Which one is better? There are advantages to both. That's why many investors own both in their portfolios."

Car Leases

"UIT terminations are like car leases. At the end of your lease, you have the option either to buy (take an in-kind distribution), roll over into a new model (a new trust series), or lease another vehicle (another trust)."

CHAPTER 6

ASSET ALLOCATION / DIVERSIFICATION

Window Panes

One financial advisor describes asset allocation by drawing a large rectangle on a yellow legal pad. He shows the illustration to his client and says:

"Imagine this rectangle is an enormous plate-glass window that covers the entire front of your house. Imagine that the children in your neighborhood are playing baseball in the street.

Now picture this: a foul ball goes through that plate-glass window. The risks would be pretty high—unacceptably high.

(He draws two vertical lines and two horizontal lines dividing the large box into nine smaller boxes.)

What you need is the traditional divided window. You still can see outside and the window lets the light in, but it diversifies the risks.

It's the same concept with investments. In the investment world, we call this style 'diversification.' Up here, you have large cap growth, and down here, you have mid cap value. Each category behaves differently in different market conditions.

Dividing your investments into each one of these styles is a little bit like switching from that plate-glass window to the traditional divided window."

Farming

"This country has been built on farming. All farmers have similar challenges of weather, land, and market. Experienced farmers deal with that unpredictability by planting a variety of crops. For example, certain crops do well one year, but not necessarily the next year. It's refreshing to see those farmers on their John Deere tractors harvesting the seven-foot corn stalks, the big tomatoes ripe on the vine, and those juicy watermelons.

These same proven principles lead to success in investing. Like farming, there's a lot of unpredictability in investing. Experienced investors deal with the uncertainty by investing in a variety of securities known to thrive in different conditions."

Rodeo

"I like to stay up at night and watch the rodeo on ESPN. In particular, I like to watch bull riding. Do you know what separates the great riders from the poor riders? Great riders rely on balance. They wrap their hand around that rope and prepare for everything and anything—and they can hold on regardless of which way the bull turns.

Bad riders don't rely on balance; they try to anticipate the bull's moves. Of course, no one can predict which way the bull will turn. So, they go down—fast and hard.

It's a little like investing. Successful investors don't try to predict which way the markets will turn; they prepare for everything and anything by balancing their portfolios. That's what I want to do for you—help bring balance to your portfolio."

Life Savers

"Edward Noble was one of those people who understood that variety is the spice of life. In 1913, he approached Clarence Crane, the inventor of the peppermint Life Saver, with the idea of producing the candy in a variety of flavors. Crane didn't want any part of this plan, and so he sold Noble all rights to the candy for $2,900.

Today, Life Savers is a $1 billion business. The reason Noble—and not Crane—became owner was because he knew the value of diversification. He didn't base his success on the sales of just one flavor of candy. He knew that by offering a variety of flavors, he could appeal to more people. At the same time, he protected his business should any one flavor fall from grace with the public."

Four-Wheel Drive

"Asset allocation is a little like four-wheel drive. If one wheel slips, you have three more opportunities for traction."

Three Little Pigs

"Remember the story of the three little pigs? If their houses were metaphors for investment portfolios, the story might go something like this:

The pig with the straw house was like a portfolio of all technology stocks in 2000. The 'big-bad-bear market' easily blew over that portfolio.

The pig with the wood house was like a portfolio made of all growth stocks. It took a little more doing, but the 'big-bad-bear market' blew it over as well.

The pig with the brick house was like a well-diversified portfolio that withstood the markets ups and downs. The market didn't blow that portfolio over. That pig was smart enough to realize that he needed the help of an electrician, a mason, and an architect to construct a house that was sturdy and strong."

Basketball Teams

"Creating a winning portfolio is a little like creating a winning basketball team.

You need defensive guards for defensive situations (bond funds), a point-guard for transitions (value funds), forwards for scoring (growth funds), and one player who can make the three-pointers (aggressive growth funds)."

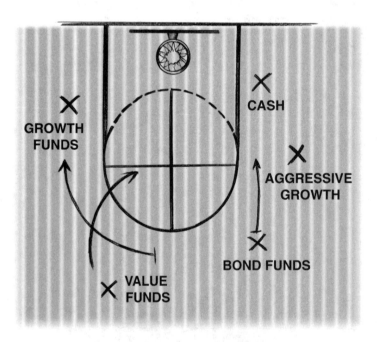

One-Club Golfers

"Every quarter an advisor in Georgia calls on clients who have made only one investment with her. She encourages them to think about a financial plan by using the analogy of a single golf club. For example, if her records indicate that a client holds just one aggressive growth fund, she'll compare it to playing 18 holes with a three-wood.

If her client holds just one CD or money market fund, she'll compare that to playing 18 holes with a putter. She then follows with, 'Why not come in so we can equip you with the right tools for your portfolio? Like golf, they can have a dramatic impact on performance.'"

Body Builder

"A portfolio's true strength comes from overall balance, not just from one or two top performers.

It's a little like the bodybuilder who focuses on just his biceps and triceps: when he is forced to lift something really heavy, his legs buckle.

Like the bodybuilder, if you focus just on growth and aggressive growth funds, your portfolio may buckle under the weight of a bear market. That's why you need to achieve balance in your portfolio."

Gretzky

When clients ask why they need to add fixed income or out-of-favor securities to their portfolios, one financial advisor responds:

"Wayne Gretzky was once asked how he had become such a great hockey player.

He replied, 'I don't skate to where the puck is, I skate to where the puck is going to be.'"

Ferris Wheel

"Markets are unpredictable. That's why we preach putting your money into many buckets, or diversification.

Like the Ferris wheel, if one bucket happens to turn upside down, all the other buckets you've invested in are still upright.

What kind of shape would you be in if all your money was in that one bucket? If one bucket goes upside down, you'd better be in the others."

(Contributed by Don Connelly)

The Financial Pyramid

"Asset allocation is a little like 'financial nutrition.' The USDA recommends apportioning your diet between breads, fruits and vegetables, milk, meat, and fats—just as I would recommend apportioning your investments between capital preservation, income, value, growth, and aggressive growth.

If you stick to just one group, you're going to get sick. Likewise, if you don't change the mix as you age, you're going to get sick. Now let's design a healthy financial plan."

Soccer Positions

"I know that you watch your grandchildren play soccer on the weekends. Think about what the coaches do with the key players: they put some on offense and some on defense—to maintain balance.

I also know at that age, the kids tend to move out of their zones and chase the ball. What happens when the defense moves too far up or the offense moves too far back? They get in trouble.

It's a lot like investing. You need a balance of offense and defense to win the game. Good investing requires experience and discipline to resist chasing the action. That's one of the values I try to add to the investment process."

Shoes in the Closet

"Allocating your money between investments is a little like buying shoes. For example, if you had $2,000 to buy shoes for the year, would you spend the whole $2,000 on one pair? (Hopefully, the answer is 'no.')

You'd probably buy casual shoes for the weekends, sneakers for exercising, formal shoes for going out, waterproof boots for the snow and rain, flip flops for the pool, and shoes of different colors and styles to match different outfits.

It's the same idea with investing. You need different securities for almost every occasion because the market conditions are constantly changing. I want you to be prepared."

Building a Portfolio with Diversified Vehicles

"Suppose I gave you a blank check to buy five vehicles. Would you buy five of the same car? Of course not.

Here's what I'd buy: a Ferrari for aggressive driving, a Mercedes for moderately aggressive driving, a Volvo for conservative driving with the kids, an SUV for all weather conditions, and a Jeep for the really bad driving conditions.

Instead of putting these vehicles in your garage, I want to put them in your portfolio. The aggressive growth fund is like the high-performance Ferrari; the growth fund is like the moderately aggressive Mercedes; the growth and income fund is a little like the conservative Volvo; the fixed-income fund is like the SUV; and the money market—with its low performance, low risk potential—is like the Jeep."

Your Retirement Plane

"If you were flying over a long distance, would you travel on a plane with one engine? How about a plane with two engines—both of which are on the right side of the plane?

Just as you need diversification and balance when flying, you need diversification and balance when investing. That's why I'm creating a financial plan that includes a balanced and diversified portfolio."

Packing for All Climates

"Suppose you got a call from your husband one day and he said, 'Honey, I've got a surprise for you. I'm taking you on a second honeymoon. Pack your bags and meet me at the airport in three hours.' Click.

What would you pack? Maybe a jacket and cold-weather clothes in case you're flying to Aspen. Or maybe a swimsuit and warm-weather clothes in case you're headed to Rio. Or maybe a windbreaker and mild-weather clothes in case you're headed for San Francisco. In the end, you'd probably pack a little of everything.

That's how I want to 'pack' your portfolio—I want you prepared for every possible climate."

One Headlight

"I'm concerned that you have only one fund in your portfolio. Did you know that you could get a ticket for driving with just one headlight? Do you know why? It's for your own safety. If you lose that headlight, you'll be driving in the dark. I think you'd agree that's a very dangerous situation.

The same can be said about investing. Driving your retirement with just one fund is dangerous. If that one fund flickers, you may have nothing left. That's why I'd suggest owning two or more funds in your portfolio."

Confidence in Your Vessel

"I know from our past visits that you enjoy fishing. Are you going to do a lot of fishing in your retirement? If so, I'd recommend investing in a good, solid boat.

Do you know why? If you fish a lot, eventually you're going to encounter a storm. What might happen if you're out in a storm and you lose confidence in your boat? You might panic and abandon ship, which is probably the most dangerous thing you could do.

That's a little like investing. If you're in the market, you're going to encounter storms once in a while. It's important that you have confidence in your investment because if you don't, you might panic and abandon ship.

That's why I'd suggest putting your money into a fund you have confidence in—one that has a number of years of experience weathering storms."

All-Star Game

"I know you're a baseball fan, and so I'd like to ask you a question: 'Do you know what happens when you don't have nine players on the field?'

In the case of one all-star game, when they ran out of pitchers it meant one thing—game over. In front of 61,000 Milwaukee fans, they ended that game in an extra-inning tie because they could not field another pitcher.

Well, baseball's a lot like investing. If you don't have all your players on the field, then your game is over. Why? Because you can't compete. If that next ball goes deep into large cap growth stocks, or deep into mid-cap value, you won't be there to catch it. You lose.

The biggest market risk you can face as an investor is not having all your players on the field."

Blending Colors

"There are over 10,000 mutual funds today. That may seem a little overwhelming at first, but not when you think about it this way: the funds are like colors.

There are three primary colors: domestic stocks, domestic bonds, and international securities. There are 50 different colors derived from those primary colors, representing 50 different categories of mutual funds. These categories are known as large cap growth funds, convertible funds, short-term government funds, and so on. There are also shades of those colors, represented by the many mutual funds within those categories.

My job is to use all of the available colors to paint a retirement plan that appeals to you and your family."

Ping-Pong Shots

"The problem with your portfolio is that it holds only one thing (CDs), which puts you at a disadvantage. Let me explain by telling you a story.

When I was a freshman in college, I used to play ping-pong on Friday nights. I had only one shot—the lob. It was a great defensive shot, but not good enough to help me keep up with the other players who had a mixture of shots for every situation—forehands, backhands, spins, and slams (in addition to the lobs). That's why they won.

That CD you're holding is a little like the lob—it's a great start, but not enough to help you keep up with the market. We need to give you a forehand, backhand, spin, and slam to win. That's what the investment pyramid is about.

The lob is a little like holding cash or CDs. The backhand, typically a defensive shot, is like fixed income securities. The forehand is both an offensive and defensive shot, which is a little like growth and income funds. The spin is an offensive shot, like growth funds. The slam is like aggressive growth funds. Are you ready to diversify your game?"

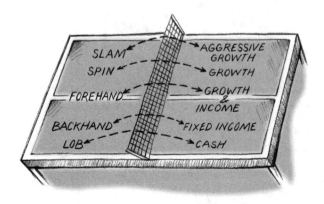

Tools for Building

"You need the right tools to build a house, just like you need the right tools to build a portfolio. For example, if you're building a house you might need a screwdriver, hammer, saw, and measuring tape in your tool belt. Could you build a house without one of these tools?

The same applies to building a portfolio. You need the right tools: money market fund, fixed income fund, growth and income fund, growth fund, and an aggressive growth fund in your financial tool belt to construct the right retirement for you."

The Portfolio Draft

One advisor uses the following analogy when advising clients to invest in funds, rather than equities:

"Individual equities are a little like football players. Few people—if any—can predict their long-term performance. For example, of the last 23 quarterbacks selected number one overall in the draft, do you know how many made it to the Pro Football Hall of Fame?

One. Terry Bradshaw. So far.

Even with all the data, research, and experts, their futures are inherently unpredictable. That's why I believe in diversification."

Breaking Pencils

"The difference between an investment and a portfolio is a little like the difference between a pencil and a group of pencils (holds up a single pencil).

I can easily break this pencil in half. But when I put the pencils together in a group (puts four or five pencils together), I cannot break them.

Investments can have similar results. A single security can break under certain market conditions, but a portfolio is exponentially stronger—if it is properly diversified."

Elevator Cables

One financial advisor explains diversification by drawing two boxes—one with a single line overhead and the other with four lines overhead. She explains:

"Do you know what these are? They're elevators—one supported by a single cable and the other supported by four cables. Which one would you rather be in during an earthquake? We need to apply the same diversification principles to your portfolio ... just in case."

Ice Skating

"Putting all your money into one stock in a volatile market can be a little like standing on a frozen pond during the spring thaw. If you're going to be out there, you should spread your weight over a large area to minimize the risks of cracking the ice. Diversification plays an even greater role in times of volatility."

"Wealthopoly"

"When you think about your long-term investments, I'd like you to think about the Monopoly board game.

When Charles Darrow invented the game back in 1934, he put the drivers of the economy around the board—railroads, utilities, and real estate.

If he had invented that game today, do you think he would have used the same industries? Probably not. He'd probably have used industries such as pharmaceuticals, technology, finance, and consumer goods.

You see, the economy and the drivers of the economy change over time. It's important that you own them for long-term growth.

That's why I'm recommending that you invest in the whole board by spreading your investments over many of these industries. That's how investors win the game."

Longwood Gardens

"I know from our previous conversations that you enjoy gardening. I'd like to tell you about my trip to Longwood Gardens in Pennsylvania.

The gardens are set up on 700 acres of land. There are roses, dogwoods, and cherry blossoms—just about everything that blooms in spring. Everywhere I turned, there was something new.

They have a staff of 600 gardeners who prune, water, and care for the flowers. They change the gardens every quarter so that they have the ideal flowers for each season.

It reminds me of our asset allocation program, which helps us select the best of all mutual funds for your portfolio. The program rebalances your allocations each and every quarter to ensure that you have the right diversification among the asset classes.

It's a buy-and-maintain approach, not a buy-and-neglect approach—just like Longwood Garden's. Using this system, we'll prune and rebalance your portfolio every quarter."

Picture Windows

"Mr. Smith and Mr. Jones have homes near a ball field. One day a powerful switch-hitting little leaguer came up and, batting right-handed, hit a ball through Mr. Smith's picture window. It cost Mr. Smith $3,000 to repair the window.

A few innings later, the same kid came up to bat again. This time, however, he was batting left-handed and hit a home run right through one of Mr. Jones' windows. The repair for Mr. Jones' window was $300.

This is why I preach diversification to my clients."

Growth in the Garden

One advisor, who is an avid gardener, shares this analogy with clients who share her hobby:

"I was having trouble getting my garden to bloom the way I'd hoped. I tried watering more often and using more fertilizer. Finally, I called a garden consultant, who immediately tested my soil. He informed me that my maintenance wasn't the problem—the soil was the problem. He explained that soil needs the right balance of acidity and alkalinity to produce growth. He started a program to bring balance back to my soil.

I see this same problem with many of my clients. Some have too much in fixed investments, while others have an overbalance of growth-type investments. Your portfolio needs balance to produce a garden you will be happy with."

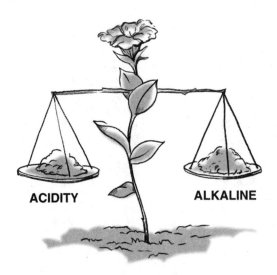

ACIDITY   **ALKALINE**

The Tool Belt

A bank broker, whose client was upset about the low rate of return on CDs, shared this analogy:

"When you are looking to get a job done, the first thing you need to check is whether you have the proper tools for the job. For example, if you have to overhaul an engine, but the only tools you have are a screwdriver and a wrench, you might eventually get the job done—but it is going to take forever.

Likewise, if your investments don't match up with your goals, you may need to look at a different set of tools. We have over 4,000 tools from which to choose."

Guitar Strings

"Investing can be a little like playing a guitar. If you want to make money at it, you'll need practice, experience, and the right equipment—or lots of luck. You also will need to play on more than just one string. You'll have to learn to use all six strings—combining the bass, mid range, and high strings—for a nice, smooth sound. Likewise, the advisor combines fixed income, equities. and international funds for a nice, smooth performance. It is also important to play in tune. Over time your guitar will need tuning—just like your portfolio will need rebalancing. If you ignore this step, it could cause some problems for your portfolio."

CHAPTER 7

PROTECTING INVESTMENTS / TAXATION

Russian Doll Set

One financial advisor has a Russian doll set on her desk. When introducing an annuity with diverse investment options, she places the doll set in front of the client and says:

"The annuity we're talking about is very much like this Russian doll set. On the surface it looks like one investment, but in fact (she starts pulling dolls out), it is many investment options rolled into one.

If you want mutual funds, they're in the annuity. If you want a guaranteed rate of return on some or all of your money, it is in the annuity. In fact, this particular annuity has X options for you to choose from—all in a tax-sheltered investment vehicle."

Frequent Flyer Miles

"Like you, I travel a lot. When I began traveling, the airlines offered me a frequent flyer account. I wavered because it takes quite awhile to earn enough miles to get a free ticket—and that's for domestic tickets. The only flight I really wanted to take with my family was to Australia, but I knew that earning so many miles would take forever. Reluctantly, I signed up for the program. I now have earned almost enough frequent flyer miles to take that trip. In hindsight, I'm really glad I did it.

It's a little like the tax-deferred investment. At first you may not think the tax savings amount to much, but over the long term, the savings can make a meaningful and measurable difference."

Cheap Sneakers

"Would you run a marathon in cheap running shoes? Of course not. You want shoes that will help you maximize efficiency so that you can run your best race. Over the long journey, good shoes are going to make a difference.

It's a little like investing. If you invest in cheap and taxable securities, they're going to make you work harder each year because of the taxes each April. Over the long run, those taxes are going to hurt your performance more and more. My advice is to take your investing as seriously as you take your running—and invest with the best vehicle you can."

The Fox and the Henhouse

One financial advisor explains the tax-deferred annuity's tax benefits this way:

"The long-term goal of investing is to multiply the eggs in our baskets. Most people are focused on producing more eggs (getting high returns) but pay little attention to the fox that perpetually robs the henhouse. If you ignore the fox, there eventually will be nobody left to produce more eggs.

That fox is taxation. The annuity I'm about to show you builds a high fence around the henhouse to keep the foxes out—which allows your eggs to multiply."

Duty-Free Store

"Annuities are a little like duty-free shops at the airport. Here's why. First, everything in the shop is exempt from taxes. Second, there's usually a wide selection of products available. Third, you have to be going on a long journey to shop there."

The "AnnuiTree"

One financial advisor explains the tax advantages to a first-time investor this way:

"Let's imagine that your back yard is like your portfolio. You haven't planted anything yet. Many years down the road you're going to retire, and one of the things you want for your retirement is a hammock in the back yard—along with a gentle breeze, lots of shade, and plenty of lemonade. So you prepare for this by planting trees in your back yard.

The problem is, as the tree grows, the IRS man shows up every April and trims back the growth by as much as four percent. In the end, you may not have enough shade for your hammock. That's why you should plant the 'AnnuiTree'—a tree that the IRS cannot touch. In fact, this tree has step-up plans and compounding features that assure growth."

The Kitchen Conversation

One financial advisor—prepared with two glasses and a water pitcher—sits down with a husband and wife. He begins by placing one glass in front of the husband and another in front of the wife:

"Sir, let's say you invest in a taxable security and, Ma'am, you invest the same amount in an annuity. (He fills both glasses half way.) Both of you now have a little growth this year. (He pours equal amounts in both glasses.)

Now, it's April 15th, and you have to pay taxes. Ma'am, you're OK because you're holding an annuity. Sir, the IRS is going to take 20 percent of your gain, so please take a sip from your glass. Hold on, some of that growth was short-term and subject to income tax rates. So, please take another sip.

OK, now another year goes by, and both of you earned some growth. (He pours equal amounts in both glasses.) It's now April 15th, and you have to pay taxes. Ma'am, you're OK, because you're holding an annuity, but, Sir, the IRS is going to take 20 percent of your gain again this year. So, please take another sip from your glass. Hold on, this year you had one mutual fund earn much more than the others, and so we've rebalanced your portfolio. It was the right thing to do, but nonetheless, it was a taxable event. Please take another sip from your glass.

Now take a look at your glasses. Assuming equal growth from both investments, who kept more? That's after just two years. Think about your long-term situation."

Lane Bumpers

"I'd like to tell you about something that happened last weekend. We had a birthday party for my four-year-old daughter. Since the kids love to bowl, we decide to have her party at the bowling alley. We invited all her friends and their parents.

I had to get the cake, the candy, and some other things, and so I showed up a little late. I walked in and everybody was mad. All the kids were stomping around because they weren't having fun. I couldn't figure out why they were miserable at my daughter's birthday party. I thought it was going to be a disaster.

When I got to my lane, this guy recognized me and said, 'I'm so glad you're here. We'll get your lanes set up for you.' So, my kids switched lanes, picked up the little bowling balls, and started rolling away. Voila! No more gutter balls. The balls bounced here, bounced there, and knocked down one or two pins. Although my kids weren't getting strikes and spares, they were high-fiving each other and having a blast!

The other kids were still having a terrible time, and pretty soon they noticed that my kids were having a pretty darned good time over here. The only difference between their lanes and ours was the use of bumper pads! The others decided they also wanted bumpers on their gutters. Soon there were bumpers on all the lanes, and everyone started having fun. Nobody wanted to leave.

On my way into work the next day, I thought about how that was a little like investing. You've got clients that are now unhappy because they've been failing. What if we gave them bumpers? Would that maybe make them happy? Would it make you happy? Would you have more fun working with your clients if they had bumpers in their gutters? Well, that's what I'm going to talk about—a variable annuity, which gives principal protection."

Guardrails

"Can you imagine crossing over the Golden Gate Bridge without guardrails? That's a little like investing without the principal protection with annuities.

Principal protection allows you to cross safely—even at higher speeds—just like the guardrails."

Modern Auto Safety

"Remember when we were little kids and our parents took us on road trips? They'd pack everyone into that 1975 full-size station wagon and take a road trip to Florida or the Grand Canyon. Do you remember how they would pack that car so full that the back bumper would scrape the road and the hood ornament would point straight up to the stratosphere?

You would have to ride next to your dad in the front seat—no air bags, child seats, or padded dashboards. Child harnesses consisted of your dad reaching across you to keep you from sliding off the vinyl seats into the dashboard.

With all the advances in safety—shoulder harnesses, air bags, and soft-impact designs, would you ever want your kids in one of those antiques? Of course not. You would want all the modern safety features.

That's a little like investing. With today's principal protection and death benefit guarantees, why would you go with an older vehicle that doesn't offer this kind of safety for you and your family?"

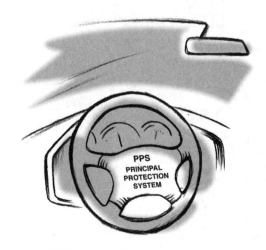

The Reset Button

"My nephews have a Play Station, and I had a chance to watch them play last weekend. Do you know what they did when they were disappointed with their performance? They hit the reset button and started over—it was that simple.

Wouldn't it be great if you could do the same with investments? Actually, you can with the annuity. We have the ability to hit a reset button to correct for some of these uncontrollable events. For instance, if your portfolio is down in value, you can hit the reset button. It will take you back to the highest anniversary value, and you can receive the income benefit from that value for the rest of your life."

Digital Camera Warranty

"Does anyone here have a family that's into photo albums? I married into one. My wife is a huge picture taker, and her family has lots of photo albums. In fact, you know those big trunks that kids take to college? She has two of them filled with photographs. She loves it, and so do I. It's special for me to see what she was like growing up.

We just had our two-year anniversary. I knew she was getting me a really nice watch, but I didn't know what to get her. Maybe a photo album? I decided instead to go for the big bucks and get her a brand-new, fancy digital video camera. I picked one out which cost quite a bit of money—$850. I went up to the counter and—if you've bought any electronic equipment lately—you know that they asked me if I'd like to purchase a warranty. Normally I'd say no, but I knew that my wife would rely on this camera and that it was important to her, especially for big occasions. By this time, it was also important to me too. After all, you only have one chance to get those memories on film. So, I agreed to purchase the warranty. I wasn't about to let something as small as a little cost of an extended warranty keep me from having these memories.

If something is valuable enough to you, you're going to want some protection. Likewise, aren't peoples' retirements valuable to them? If you could show your clients how to add protection to their retirement accounts, it seems to me that it would be an easy decision."

Swimsuit

"It has always been my dream to build a pool in my backyard. It's so hot in California that having a pool is just the greatest. The downside to a private pool is that we've been hearing horror stories about children having accidents—and we have a three-year-old girl. She's a free spirit, which causes us to be even more concerned for her safety.

It took a wonderful friend of ours to tell us about a great new invention—a bathing suit with a built-in inner tube. It's stylish—with bears and little Hawaiian prints and so we know she'll wear it. But, here's the payoff: it gives us the peace of mind of knowing that if she's in the pool, and we turn our heads for a second or something diverts our attention, she'll still be protected.

That's like what we are able to offer investors. Regardless of whether it's living benefits or death benefits, we're able to give people the opportunity to invest in the market with protection and peace of mind."

Roller Coaster

"When I was six years old, my father took us to Six Flags in St. Louis. We spent the morning at the water park and on the kiddy rides. My father soon tired of that. He said, 'Son, we're going on the Screaming Eagle.'

'Whoa, Screaming Eagle!' Let me paint a little picture for you. The roller coaster probably takes up a good eighth of the park and is very intimidating. I was scared to death—I was kicking and screaming the whole way and crying, 'I don't want to go! No! No!' But, he calmly lifted me up and put me in the roller coaster.

Suddenly the safety bar came down, and I began to feel a little better. My dad was sitting next to me holding my hand, and the bar was holding me in place so I couldn't move. I knew then that I couldn't fall out. We went up and down and all over. By the end of the ride, I had a huge smile on my face.

Many investors have been on a financial roller coaster. Their experience gives an opportunity for advisors to be like my dad: to sit next to their clients and give them safety harnesses. After all, without that harness, investors may want to get off this ride because they could get hurt. That protection is what the annuity gives them."

Guaranteed Par

"If you were invited to play in a major golf tournament, would you play conservatively or aggressively? If I were playing in a televised golf tournament with the likes of Phil Mickelson and Tiger Woods, I'd play pretty conservatively.

What if you were given an advantage in this tournament? What if you were guaranteed par, and any shots over par would not count? Would that change your strategy? Would you be a little more aggressive? Would you be a little more relaxed in your game? Could you afford to take more risks?

What if I could help you do the same thing with your clients' investments? First, we'd identify 'par,' which right now is about five to six percent annual return. Then, we could establish a more aggressive strategy to help them reach for the higher returns of 10 or 11 percent. Do you think this advantage would help your clients be a little more aggressive and a little more relaxed?"

Pitons

One advisor uses a piton (used for rock climbing) to explain the variable annuity's step-up provision. Holding up the piton and a carabiner, he begins:

"I'd like to explain the step-up provision with the help of this tool. Do you know what this is? It's a safety device called a piton, which costs about $8.50. Mountain climbers use this tool when they scale cliffs. They pound this end into the rocks every few feet and then thread their safety ropes through this little hole. If they slip, they'll fall only as far as the highest piton. It's a no brainer for mountain climbers—they don't skimp on these devices.

We have the same safety device for annuities, called the step-up provision. As your investments grow in value, your step up provision also rises. That way, if the market slips, your portfolio will fall only as far as the highest step. Like pitons, they're not free—but, for a small cost, you can avoid a serious injury."

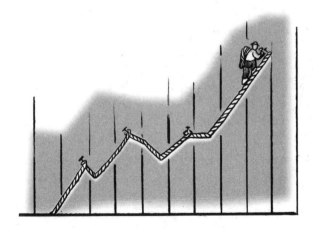

Uncle Sam and the Angel Food Cake

"About a year ago, I had the entire family over for Thanksgiving dinner. I made my specialty—angel food cake. I mixed all the ingredients together and put the cake in the oven. My family and I then went out for a walk, except there was one person left in the house—my uncle, Sam.

Sam didn't go for the walk with the rest of the family because he was upstairs sleeping. But when we left, Sam woke up. He smelled the cake baking in the oven, and so he walked down to the kitchen. He opened the oven door to see what smelled so good—and the heat escaped. A few minutes later, he opened that door—and again, some of the heat escaped. He opened that oven door four times!

When we returned from our walk, I checked on the cake. It was only five inches high—and it was supposed to be twice that high! Now I didn't have enough to feed my entire family! But you know what? I had no one to blame but myself because I knew that Uncle Sam would open that door—he always does!

We have investments that are a little like an oven door that locks Uncle Sam out. These investments include annuities, retirement accounts, and municipal bonds."

Leaks

"Investment portfolios are a little like scuba tanks—leaks can have serious consequences. If you're diving and your tank is leaking air, your dive is going to get cut short.

The same is true of investing. If your portfolio has a tax leak, your retirement could get cut short—and you might have to go back to work.

I can show you how to seal the tax leak with investment planning, and so you'll keep as much of your gains as possible."

Aerodynamic Tax Returns

"Cars are a little like investments—the higher the performance, the greater the resistance. With cars, the wind resistance increases in proportion to your speed. With investments, the tax burden increases in proportion to your gains. But, there are solutions.

With cars, it's aerodynamics—engineered to help slice through the wind. With investments, it's tax-exempt investments—designed to slice your tax burden."

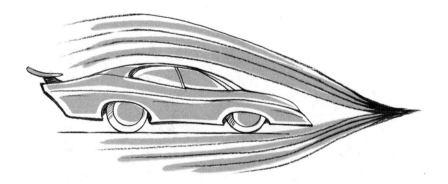

Marathons

"Investing for retirement can be a little like running a marathon—you want to avoid as many obstacles as you can. In marathons, hills and headwinds will slow your performance. In investing, federal and state taxes will slow your performance.

I can show you how to invest without those hills and headwinds, and so you'll reach your goals much quicker."

Racing Performance

"My father retired. No, he's not spending time on golf courses, cruises, or in the garden—he's racing Ferraris. I asked him his strategy for winning.

He said that the number one factor is the efficiency of the car—the calibration of the spoiler, the right tires, and the proper fuel mixture. He cleans, waxes, and polishes every square inch of the car. He also fills in the dents and dings—eliminating any drag on the aerodynamics—because these races are won or lost by hundredths of a second. He ekes every bit of efficiency out of the car.

How does this relate to your investments? I'd like to make your portfolio as efficient as possible by reducing the drag of taxes on your performance. It could help put you in the winner's circle."

Ski Tuning

"Let me explain tax-efficient investing by way of a ski analogy. My wife and I like to ski. Five years ago, we bought our equipment and have been skiing ever since. This year, I noticed something: my wife is faster than I. Do you know why? Because she tunes her skis. Every season she takes them to the ski shop to fill in the scratches and grooves from the rocks and twigs on the slopes. Her skis have smooth bottoms, and so there's no resistance. My skis have scratches, dings, and holes, which create a lot of resistance. I have to ski harder and take more risks just to keep up with my wife.

Those cuts and grooves on the bottom of my skis are a little like the taxes on your portfolio—they slow you down and make you work harder to keep up. Let me show you how to 'tune' your portfolio with tax-efficient investments."

Shark Cage

"My wife and I were fortunate enough to take our honeymoon in Australia. I was young enough to think, 'Hey, let's try scuba diving for the first time.' So, after much discussion, we decided to give it a try.

As we were boating out to the dive sight, I was reminded of Jaws, and I began having second—and third—thoughts.

Finally the captain said, 'If you want peace of mind, we can let you have a shark cage for a small extra fee.'

I asked, 'What does a shark cage buy you?'

He answered, 'It buys you protection. You can still enjoy the ride and see all the beautiful fish under the sea—but you're surrounded by a cage to protect you from the outside and from shark attacks.'

As I was down in the water taking pictures of all the beautiful fish and the coral reef, wham! I was hit from behind! Believe it or not, a shark brushed up against my cage. Trust me, you can hear someone scream underwater. I then remembered the cage around me and knew everything was going to be OK. I finished the dive and left feeling fulfilled.

Scuba diving is a little like investing. Sometimes things get a little too exciting. During those times, you need a little extra protection. That's why I recommend municipal bonds with AAA-rated insurance. Like the shark cage, it can make the difference when things get dangerous."

(Contributed by Robyn Lewis)

Lump-Sum Rollover

"The option to take a lump sum in cash is kind of like getting the wrong haircut at the barber shop. Depending on the size of the check, it can cause you to jump up as much as two tax brackets. In addition, there may be mandatory withholding—not to mention the balance of taxes due—and the possible ten percent penalty.

After all is said and done, it can be very expensive. I often say that it's like going to the barber shop, asking for a trim, and coming out with a Mohawk. This is your Mohawk."

(Contributed by Robyn Lewis)

CHAPTER 8

THE TIME TO INVEST

Easing into the Water

"Jumping into an investment is a little like jumping into a pool. Some people like to jump right in—full and immediate! Others like to use the stairs—and get acclimated to the water a little bit at a time.

You have the same option with investing. You can make a lump-sum investment and put all your money to work at once. Or, you can use our dollar cost averaging plan to ease into the market a little bit at a time."

Splitting from the Herd

"Contrarian investing can offer potential rewards, but it's also packed with risks. It's kind of like the zebras who wander away from their herds. When zebras travel alone, they graze on grass that is not trampled and muddy and breathe air that is fresh and not dusty. But when predators approach, they are alone and unprotected—and the consequences can be swift and unforgiving."

The Only Check to Bounce

"One fellow said that he thought the perfect retirement plan would be one where the only check that bounced was the one written to his undertaker.

Unfortunately, most of us have no idea how long we're going to live. If you're 50 years old today, there's a good chance you'll be around 36 more years. We need to make sure your money is around as long as you are. For that to be possible, you must begin investing now."

The Measuring Tape

"One financial advisor has a drawer of 72-inch measuring tapes, which he uses in his presentations to clients. Here is an example of one of his presentations:

'At what age do you want to retire?'

Client replies, 'At age 65.'

(The advisor pulls out a measuring tape and scissors, cuts the tape at 65 inches, and lets the tape roll out to the floor.)

He then asks, 'How old are you today?'

Client replies, '51 years old.'

(The financial advisor then cuts the tape at 51 inches, lets the large part of the tape fall to the floor, and holds the 14 inches from 51 to 65 inches.)

The advisor says, 'That's over and done with' (points to tape on the floor). 'This is what we have to work with' (points to tape in his hand). 'We have some serious investment work to do from now until 65.'

The advisor says, 'You can keep this as a reminder' (hands the 14-inch tape to his client)."

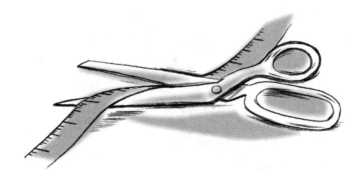

Paychecks

"After calculating the amount his client will need to retire, one advisor asks his clients: 'At what age do you want to retire?'

Client replies, 'Age 65.'

Advisor asks, 'How old are you now?'

Client replies, '45.'

Advisor asks, 'How much do you make a year?'

Client responds, '$50,000.'

Advisor says, 'OK, if my math is correct, you have 240 monthly paychecks left in your working career. According to our previous discussion, you need $500,000 to draw from at retirement. Today you have $140,000. We're $360,000 shy right now. What is the likelihood that you will have saved $1,500 toward retirement out of each of your last 240 checks?'

Client answers, 'Not likely.'

Advisor says, 'Then, here is the plan we'll need to follow to get you there ...'

The advisor then gives an illustration of investments and rate of return to reach the client's retirement goal."

Moving into the Market

"I tell people that now the market is low, which is the best time to get into the market—but clients have heard that forever. How do you stress that urgency?

So I began asking people in my group presentations, 'Who here has refinanced?' (Several hands will go up.)

I then ask, 'Why?'

Someone answers, 'Because the rates are low.'

I ask, 'Well, why not wait until next week, next month, or next year?'

The response is always, 'Because rates may go up and I want to get in on the low rates.'

I say, 'Isn't the same true now of the market?'"

CHAPTER 9

LONG-TERM
PERSPECTIVES

Steadfast Training

"Let me tell you a story about a set of identical twins who trained for a triathlon.

Both the brothers were disciplined and trained hard. One cold, rainy day, they both pulled muscles as they were training. One brother nursed the pulled muscle back to health and soon was back to his full regimen. But the other brother gave up out of fear that he would reinjure that muscle. He stayed on the sidelines while his brother fulfilled his dream of entering and finishing that race.

It reminds me of investors. Everyone has goals and dreams and almost everyone has been hurt to some degree by the market over the last few years. I encourage all of my clients to be like the first brother—to continue with their regimen and not lose sight of their goals."

(Contributed by Robyn Lewis)

Mark McGwire

"Let me tell you a story about 'nine to seventy in four.' Do you know how many home runs Mark McGwire had in 1993? Nine. Do you know how many he had in 1994? Nine. Three years later, Oakland traded him to St. Louis; the following year, he broke the record with 70 home runs.

My point is that performance can turn around rather quickly. If you give up too early, you may lose out on a record performance. That's why you should consider getting off the fence and back into the market."

Getting Out of Rough Seas

"A couple of years ago, I went on a scuba diving vacation to Cozumel, Mexico. We went on a group dive, and just as we went underwater, the surface conditions started to change: clouds began to roll in; the swells rose to about three or four feet high; and the water became very choppy.

As I was swimming back to the boat, I noticed the couple in front of me were not experienced divers, and so I offered to help them into the boat. They were kind of snobby about it and were determined to do it themselves. Sure enough, the lady tried to get on that boat at the bottom of a swell. As she pulled herself up, the boat jumped three or four feet and caught her in the face. She lost two teeth and broke her nose.

I'm telling you this story for two reasons. First, it's always a good idea to accept help from someone more experienced than you. And second, sometimes getting out can be more dangerous than staying in.

It's a little like investing. Inexperienced investors have abandoned the markets because they were too choppy, but in the long run, they may be hurting themselves more by getting out."

Facing the Bear

"If you ever come in contact with a bear, keep a cool head and try to stay calm—do not yell, scream, kick, or fight. Make no sudden moves, stand your ground, and do not try to outrun a bear—it will only make matters worse.

My advice is to stay the course—stay invested, focus on long-term goals, and look for the opportunities."

The Best Time to Jump in the Markets

One advisor has clients who want to invest only when the market is up—never when the market is down. She offers them the story of the Acapulco cliff diver.

"When the diver was asked how he survived cliff diving for so long, he responded: 'I know from experience when to dive in. You can see the water at the bottom of the cliffs rise and fall with the currents. When the tide is out, the water is too shallow. One-time cliff divers jump when they see the water at its crest. However, by the time they land, the tide is out and the water is too shallow. Me, I wait until the tide is out and I can see the rocks. That's when I dive in. By the time I land, the tide is in and the water is at its crest.'

That's a little like investing. Novices buy at high tide, but experienced investors buy when they see the rocks."

Michael Jordan's Stats

"Let me give you an example of just how deceptive short-term performance can be.

Michael Jordan's career average with the Bulls was 31.5 points per game. Not once in his career did he score 31.5 points in a game! His short-term performances ranged from 12 points against Atlanta in the 1991-1992 season to 69 points against Cleveland in the 1990-1991 season. Short-term performance can be a poor indicator of long-term averages."

Meaningful Measurements

"How many inches are there between your house and my office? Of course, that's a ridiculous question. It's more appropriate to measure long distances in miles, not inches.

The same is true of investing. You can't measure the performance of your holdings by its daily or quarterly fluctuations. It's more appropriate (and more meaningful) to measure it by the mile."

The Brick

One financial advisor who kept a brick on his desk would tell his new clients:

"If the market goes down, you'll be upset—maybe so upset you'll want to throw this brick through my window. But before you do, I want you to do one thing. Write a check to your mutual fund company and tie it to this brick because when the market falls, you should be thinking about buying more shares."

(Note: You may want to hand them a self-addressed envelope rather than a brick.)

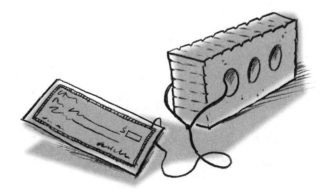

The Yo-Yo and the Hill

"Picture a man walking over hill and dale with a yo-yo. The yo-yo represents the level of the market. If you focus on the yo-yo going up and down the string, you may lose sight of how high the hill is.

Although watching the short-term performance can be entertaining, it's the long-term performance that counts."

Waves and Tides

"The ups and downs of the stock market are a little like the ocean. You have short-term volatility (waves) and longer-term trends (the tide). The waves in the financial market may be pretty low right now, but if you look at the long term trend, the tide is still pretty high. We're still in high tide."

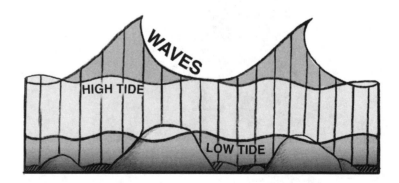

Sticking with a Winner

"I know we've made some investments recently that have fallen in value, and you're thinking about liquidating them. I'd like to suggest that we take a different course of action.

I know from our past visits that you're a baseball fan. Do you remember Ted Williams, the left fielder for the Sox? This fund—like Ted Williams—has offered extraordinary long-term performance. Liquidating this fund now would be like benching Williams when he was 0 - 4 on opening day. You should give the fund a chance to do what it's designed to do—provide long-term performance."

Livestock

"Some people think that when a stock loses money, investors are losing money, which is not always the case. Let me explain by the way of an analogy.

Suppose you own 100 head of cattle—90 heifers and 10 bulls. Today's market price is $10 a head, and so your herd is worth a total of $1,000. What would happen if you left those cattle alone for five years and didn't sell any of them? Those heifers would give birth to calves. In five years' time, you might have 400 head of cattle. Even if the market price were to decline by half, you'd still have $2,000—double your money. If that market price held at $10, you'd have $4,000 in cattle, which is a nice profit.

Just like the livestock give birth to new calves, mutual fund distributions create new shares. The dividends and capital gains earned by the fund are reinvested back into the fund (buying more shares of the fund). Even if the value of that investment declines a little bit, shareholders who reinvest may still be earning money."

The Power of a Pawn

"To the amateur, the pawn is the least valuable piece on the chessboard. The experienced player doesn't regard just the present value of the pawn, but the potential value. A pawn, if properly navigated over the course of the game, can one day become a queen or any other valuable piece.

So it is with your investment. No matter how small it may seem today, if you stay invested and navigate patiently, your investment can one day become extremely valuable."

Dollar Cost Averaging

"Moving into the market is kind of like getting into a swimming pool. Picture this: you are on vacation at a lovely resort hotel. You walk outside and approach the pool. Instead of jumping straight in, you stick your big toe in the pool to get an idea of how the water feels. Then you walk around to the ladder or steps and go down into the water at a pace you are comfortable with. Eventually, you get all the way into the pool, but you do so at a pace you are comfortable with.

Dollar cost averaging helps you get into the market ... at a pace you are comfortable with."

(Contributed by Robyn Lewis)

Marathon Training

"I find many parallels between my marathon training and investing for the long run. To run marathons, I must have fitness, endurance, and resilience. To develop fitness, I do shorter runs and lift weights. To develop endurance, I do long runs. To develop resilience, I train in all types of weather because I never know what the weather will be on the day of the run.

In investing, we need instruments that take advantage of short-term opportunities as well as investments that endure over longer time frames. It's important to invest in all weather patterns—so we don't sabotage all the work we've already done."

CHAPTER 10

THE IMPACT OF INFLATION

A Modern Tale About Rip Van Winkle

"Do you remember Rip Van Winkle? He was the one who slept for 20 years. Suppose Rip had fallen asleep 20 years ago with a dollar in his pocket. How much do you think that dollar would have been worth when he woke up? About 44 cents. Put another way, the year he fell asleep, he'd have been able to buy two cups of coffee. Today, if he ordered a caffe latte, he'd be short $2.15. The fact is, every dollar that you don't have invested will get eaten up by inflation.

Past performance is no guarantee of future results."

Football Salaries

"I understand that your goal is to have $1 million set aside for retirement. By today's standards, that might be enough for a comfortable living. How far do you think that money will go 20 or 30 years from now?

Take for example the 1972 Miami Dolphins—the only team to earn a perfect 17-0 record. Do you know how much those players earned in 1972? In the post-season, they earned $23,500 each, which was double most of their annual salaries—and they were the champions! Today, the minimum salary for an NFL rookie is $225,000, and for a ten-year veteran, it's $750,000.

That's the impact of inflation over time—and that's why it is a big factor in retirement income planning."

Golfing Against the Wind

"A few weeks ago a good friend of mine invited me to his country club for a round of golf. Both of us had great drives off the first tee and were about 250 yards off the green. We pulled out our irons, and I landed on the green about 20 yards from the hole. Sean also had an excellent shot, but when his ball was about halfway to the green, a headwind came out of nowhere and stopped his ball in mid-flight, landing in a hazard. Although Sean is a much better golfer, I won the hole because of that headwind.

It reminds me a little of your situation. You're investing against a headwind called inflation. It makes you work a little harder to reach the green, but with proper planning, you can adjust your approach so you don't double bogie your retirement."

Walking Up the Down Escalator

"Planning for retirement is a little like walking up the down escalator. The escalator is moving at the rate of inflation. If you just stand still and do nothing with your money, you will actually move backwards—farther from your goal. If you climb too slowly with ultra-conservative investments, you may still move backward—getting farther from retirement. To make any progress at all toward retirement, you need to climb faster than the rate of inflation."

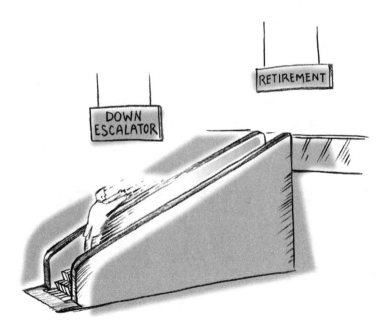

A First-Class Stamp

"A simple way to see the effects of inflation is to look at postage stamps and the bills you attach to them. In 1983, it cost you 20¢ to mail in your monthly payment. In 2003, it cost you 37¢. The increase in postage alone is 85 percent. Add to that how much more you are now sending to the electric company, the cable company, and so on, and you see the effects of inflation. What will these things cost in the year 2013? Certainly much more than they do today. That's why your money needs to grow—just to break even."

CHAPTER 11

INVESTMENT
BASICS

Mulching

"I have a friend who lives in a beautiful mansion. The first thing people notice about his estate is the plush lawn—it's perfect. I asked him if he and his four kids spend day and night making the lawn look that great.

He explained that he uses a mulching lawn mower, which recycles the grass clippings back into the lawn. In other words, the clippings act as a fertilizer that compounds the growth of the lawn.

It's a little like investing. If you reinvest your interest, dividends, and gains, you earn compound growth—growth on growth. It's kind of like mulching your portfolio. But if you're in taxable investments, Uncle Sam takes some of those clippings—which can't be reinvested for compounded growth. It's a little like bagging the grass and putting it out for the trash, rather than putting it back into the lawn."

Selecting Tires

"Selecting mutual funds for your portfolio is a little like selecting tires for your car. You can get tires with minimal tread for dry road conditions, deep tread for wet conditions, or large, knobby tires for off-road conditions. When selecting investments, you can get aggressive growth funds for ideal market conditions, growth and income funds for mixed conditions, or fixed income funds for adverse conditions.

This equity and income fund is a little like the all-weather tire—suitable for diverse market conditions."

Grocery Shopping

"Stocks, mutual funds, and portfolios are a little like grocery shopping. When you go to the store, you buy some Kelloggs, Proctor & Gamble, Nabisco,. and General Mills (stocks). When you go to the checkout, they put your groceries in bags (mutual funds). When you put the bags into a cart, that's your portfolio. This simple method keeps your investments organized and manageable."

Your Money and Your Life

"There are only four possible outcomes with respect to your life and your money: one is tragic; two are unavoidable; and the fourth is what we're planning for."

(The advisor draws four boxes, labels them as below, and explains that a financial plan should prepare them for box number two—alive and with money.)

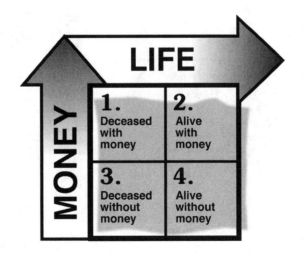

College Courses and Degrees

One financial advisor points to his degree hanging on the wall and says:

"In a way, that diploma on the wall is a great metaphor for the difference between individual securities and mutual funds or unit trusts. Individual securities are a little like a college course—very specific and focused on a single topic. Funds and trusts are more like the degree—comprised of many courses broadly related to the topic. The way I look at it, a degree better prepares you for the future."

INDIVIDUAL SECURITIES

MUTUAL FUNDS

Building a Pyramid for Your Assets

"Building a solid portfolio is very much like building the pyramids of long ago. Ancient Egyptians built pyramids for keeping the family treasures—designed to stand the test of time.

That's why we're going to look at an asset allocation plan that has stood the test of time. The asset groups I will show you today have returned an average of X percent over an XX-year period. I think your family treasures need the same sort of care and protection that pyramids provided in ancient times. Here's how we'll build your pyramid ..."

Gambling Versus Investing

"Some people compare investing to gambling, but the opposite actually is closer to the truth. Have you ever gambled at a casino? If you have, you probably know that the odds are in favor of the house (called the 'house edge'). Statistically, the longer you gamble, the greater your chances are of losing money.

Just the opposite is true of investing. Statistically, the longer you invest, the greater your chances are of making money. For example, over the last 74 years, investors who held their investments for just one year had positive returns 70 percent of the time; those who held for five years had positive returns 91 percent of the time; and those who held for ten years had positive returns 98 percent of the time."

Microwave Popcorn

"Mutual funds are a little like microwave popcorn. The popcorn and butter are premeasured by the experts, and there's no oil to add. Just pop the bag into the microwave and enjoy—everything's done for you.

Of course, there's no such thing as the perfect bag of popcorn. Some of those kernels shoot through to the top, settle back to the bottom and burn. Others don't pop at all. But the majority pop perfectly, which helps you build wealth over time."

Perennials

"Enrolling in a mutual fund's automatic reinvestment is a little like planting perennials. The roots from the first plant give birth to more plants each year. Before long, you have a garden full of flowers."

Winter Crops

John Santi, an advisor in Memphis, shared this story with a client, whom he discovered had grown up on a farm.

"Growing up, did you ever hear of anyone who tried to plant summer crops in the winter? No. But what did people expect in the winter? Garlic and winter wheat—crops designed to grow in that climate.

Some would say that stocks are summer crops and that this is not the season to be planting. We need to research investment crops that flourish in the season we are in now."

How the Market Prices Stocks

"It has been said that the market is a barometer, not a thermometer. What does that mean? It means the price of a stock today is not established by 'taking the temperature' of that company today but by anticipating the temperature of that company tomorrow. The market looks at the barometric pressures on the company and tries to anticipate how they will affect the temperature a month from now and a year from now.

Wall Street, in many ways, acts like a weatherman. Our opportunities for gain come from being able to recognize when the weatherman is wrong about a certain company."

There Goes the Neighborhood

An advisor, a former realtor, likes to share this analogy.

"Understanding when to sell a stock or fund is kind of like knowing when to sell a home. Say, for instance, you hear a rumor that a juvenile detention center is going to be built just down the road—you may want to sell before depreciation sets in.

On the other hand, if you hear that a state-of-the-art elementary school is going to be built, you may want to wait for the property to appreciate and then sell.

I look at my job as a sort of 'neighborhood watch.' I keep my eye on developments in the particular industries in which you are invested. If I advise you to sell, it is because I see a bad influence moving into the neighborhood."

CHAPTER 12

INVESTMENT
WISDOM

Dead Reckoning

"I know from our past conversations that you enjoy boating. So, I'd like to explain what I do by the way of an analogy and a question. Do you know how beginners navigate? It's called dead reckoning. They use a compass, point their boat west, and hope to hit land.

Novice investors do the same thing with their portfolios. They invest in a few securities, forget about them, and hope the investments grow before they reach retirement. In fact, more than a few people have told me that they haven't been opening their retirement fund statements because they're afraid to look. These people are 'dead reckoning' their retirements.

I navigate financial portfolios using GPS (Global Positioning System). I monitor where you are at any given time and compare it to where you want to be. If market changes force you off course, I'll call you, and we'll adjust. But don't let that scare you. We know that markets will force you off course from time to time—just like the ocean currents and winds force ships off course. Keeping you on course is what you can expect from me as your advisor."

Eluding the Bears

"Protecting yourself in bear markets is a little like protecting yourself from the real thing—bears.

When you're deep in bear country, you need to take preventative measures such as preparing food away from camp and storing groceries in bags hung from trees. If you wait until you see the bear, it's probably too late.

We can help you take preventative measures with asset allocation tools and annuities—all designed to help you reach your destination while protecting you in bear markets."

Remote Controls

"Over the years I've added new components to my home entertainment system—screen-in-screen TV, DVD player, CD player, VHS, tuner, Play Station, and cable box—and it's awesome! But there's a problem: there are six remote controls, which is a little unwieldy. I'm the only one who knows how to work the whole system. So if anything happens to me, my family won't be watching TV for a long, long time.

The entertainment system is kind of like some investment accounts I see. Over time, people add IRAs, 401(k)s, stocks, and annuities—all in different places—which is unwieldy and uncontrollable. If something happens to them, their families will have their hands full trying to make sense of everything.

This leads me to one of the most important services we offer—consolidating your accounts for more control."

Bad Nutrition

"I want you to close your eyes and pretend it's morning. You wake up and devour four strips of bacon, three eggs cooked in bacon fat, grits prepared with a half stick of butter, and coffee—this is your breakfast every morning. Now, I want you to think 20 years down the road. What do you look like? How do you feel? What health problems have evolved?

Investing in the wrong things can have the same consequences. You may not feel it today or tomorrow, but it will catch up to you. If you put all of your money in one stock or one asset class, it can mean bad financial nutrition over time. This is why the occasional 'fiscal checkup' can help from time to time."

Hot Air Ballooning

"Good balloonists—those with experience and extensive knowledge of the wind patterns—can usually make their way to any given destination. Of course, ballooning is not a flight of precision—it requires constant adjustments.

Ballooning is a little like investing. Experienced investors know that equity markets are not always 'blowing north at 15 miles per hour,' and so they study the patterns and learn how to adjust their investment portfolios to the shifting conditions."

Planting a Seed

"Have you ever planted a seed and forgotten to water it? If you have, you realize that there's more work to growing beautiful flowers than just dropping a seed in the ground. When the ground's dry, we water it. When it's cold, we protect it.

Some advisors will show you a pretty picture of a flower, drop your investment seed in the ground, and then forget about it. Around here we believe that it's what we do after we plant the seed that matters."

Burnt Apple Pie

"What happens if you forget about the apple pie baking in the oven? It burns.

The same thing can happen to your portfolio. If we leave a portfolio in the market for too long and forget about it, bad things can happen. That's why I keep an eye on all the securities that I recommend. It's also why I ask my clients to schedule appointments every X months so that we can reassess their portfolios."

Investments for Life

"I've driven many miles over the years—fifty to sixty thousand miles a year—going from appointment to appointment. I took it for granted but always played it safe. In fact, I never had a speeding ticket or an accident—not even a scratch. All that changed last year when I was driving to Portland, Maine. Everything was going along just beautifully when all of a sudden, the traffic came to a screeching halt. I was the last in a line of bumper-to-bumper traffic. The problem was, the guy behind me didn't see the stopped traffic and hit me—at about 60mph. My car was totaled, and I was in pretty bad shape. Because driving is how I make a living, I eventually had to get behind the wheel again. So, I decided to buy a new car—a white Volvo station wagon. Volvo's slogan is: 'Volvo for life.' Like any other car, Volvo gets you from point A to point B—but it gets you there safely.

The reason I'm telling you this story is because we've seen a great many accidents in the equity markets over the years. There have been turbulent times—and people have been hurt. Just like I didn't want to get back in the car again, many investors don't want to get back in the market.

In this market, investors want those extra safety features to help them gain the confidence to get back on the road to retirement. Our annuity product line comes with the most features—and with the biggest guarantees in the industry."

Batting Singles and Doubles

"Successful portfolios are a little like successful baseball teams—winning strategies focus on singles and doubles, not on grand slams."

Financial Fitness

"Investing is a little like exercise—you can't get healthy with a few abdominal exercises. It takes discipline, a strict diet, and diversity of exercise over a meaningful and measurable period of time.

The same is true of investing. Financial fitness can happen only with a disciplined investment process, diversification, and market appreciation over a meaningful period of time. I'm kind of like a personal trainer for your portfolio."

SUN Morning Walk
MON Workout on Weights
TUES Salad & Fruit Day
WED Evening walk
THUR Yoga class
FRI Basketball
SAT Tennis 7:00 AM

Confidence in Your Vessel

"I know from our past conversations that you enjoy fishing. Are you going to do a lot of fishing in your retirement? If so, I'd recommend investing in a good, solid boat. If you fish a lot, eventually you're going to encounter a storm. If you lack confidence in your boat, you might panic and abandon ship—which is probably the most dangerous thing you could do.

Likewise, if you're in the market, you're going to encounter some storms. It's important that you have confidence in your investment, because if you don't, you might panic and abandon ship—which is one of the most dangerous things you can do. That's why I'd suggest putting your money into a fund in which you have confidence—a fund that has a number of years of experience weathering storms."

Famous Names

"What does Bush have in common with Grant, Jackson, Monroe, Roosevelt, and Washington? They're all automobile companies that went out of business in the 1920's. Back then, there were over 250 car companies in business. Today, there are only a handful.

This scenario is typical of the great technological revolutions of our time: telegraph, railroad, telephone, radio, TV, and internet. Each invention began with hundreds of startups that have evolved into a few industry leaders.

Had you invested in any one of these industries, you'd have profited from some of the greatest inventions of our time. Had you invested in just one company, chances are you'd have a tragic story to share with your grandchildren. The advantage of mutual funds is that they offer a combination of opportunity with diversification."

"Seasonality" of Investing

"In the past, I've met many investors who did not understand the 'seasonality' of their investments. I've seen too many people who want to uproot their trees in the middle of winter; consequently, they never prosper. With just a little patience, they would have seen the season change and new growth appear.

I view your portfolio as a valuable growing tree. My job is to know when to water (buy), when to harvest (sell), when to fertilize (buy), and when to prune (sell). With patience and care, your tree will grow strong and fruitful."

Running Pace

"The economy is a little like the marathon runner who is in great shape but can't pace herself. She's in the habit of speeding up to a pace that is unsustainable. She slows down, catches her breath, regains her strength, and continues. Sometimes it takes only a mile or two to regain her strength—but sometimes it takes longer."

Traffic Jam

"Imagine that you had to drive from New York City to Los Angeles. You're in downtown Manhattan hopelessly stuck in traffic, and you see bicycle messengers whizzing past you. You jump out of your car, sell your car on the spot (at a ridiculously low price), buy a bicycle, and continue your trip to the West Coast.

As absurd as this scenario sounds, investors do this every day when they make short-term decisions for long-term journeys. Stick with a vehicle that will take you to the end of the road."

(Contributed by Don Connelly)

The Right Reaction

"Investors have drifted off the track to retirement (which happens). The critical issue is how investors react. It's a little like driving. If you drift off the side of the road and suddenly find one tire on the gravel, the worst thing you can do is panic and yank the wheel the other way. The best reaction is to hold your course and slowly move back on to the road. It can make the difference between having an accident and avoiding one.

When the markets take an unexpected turn, investors need to stay calm, hold the course, and gradually look to get back on course."

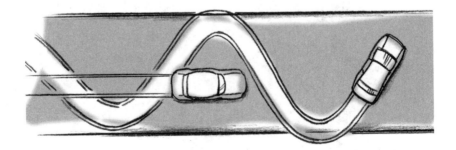

The Right Response

"Do you know who William Murdoch is? He was the First Officer aboard the Titanic. He ordered the ship's engines to be stopped, then full stern, and then hard starboard. His maneuver was probably a common-sense reaction at the time—but on closer examination, it may have been worse then doing nothing. A direct impact may have spared some of the airtight compartments.

It's a little like panic selling in bear markets. Sometimes the common-sense reaction to sell in down markets can make matters worse while staying the course can be the best option."

Rear-View Mirror

"Investors are often biased by total returns—they want to put their money into top-performing funds. But that's all based on past performance. It's like driving down the highway looking in the rear-view mirror. My job is to make them turn around, look forward, and invest for the long road ahead."

Titanic

"You should never get complacent about market risks. When the sailing looks smooth and your portfolio seems unsinkable, that's when the icebergs emerge over your bow. Don't 'Captain Smith' your portfolio—always maintain a disciplined approach to diversification and asset allocation."

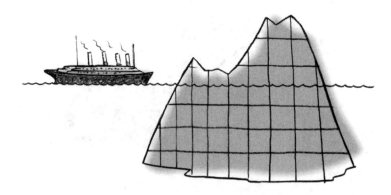

The "Retirement" Green Jacket

"The Masters has been played almost every year since 1934. In that time, there have been nine players to score a hole-in-one, but none of them went on to wear the coveted green jacket. Only those players who played consistently well during every round won.

The same principles hold true for successful investing. You can't achieve your financial goals with one or two great stocks. You need a mix of aggressive and defensive securities to get those long-term, consistent results that can help you win the game. That's how you win the 'retirement' green jacket."

Edison

"Do you know who invented the light bulb? Thomas Alva Edison is widely credited with the modern version.

Do you know how he made his money? Not from the light bulb, but from powering the light bulb—he founded the Edison Electric Company.

That's why I like investment portfolios. Managers often look at the bigger pictures when it comes to new technologies and invest in direct and indirect opportunities. The portfolios allow you to broaden your participation in the new opportunities.

By the way, do you know where Edison made his mistake? In 1892, he sold all of his interests in the Edison Electric Company when the name was changed to General Electric."

Roller Coasters

"Every day I hear people comparing today's investment market to roller coasters—and they're right. It's a pretty fair comparison if you know something about roller coasters.

At the beginning of the century, roller coasters were pretty slow. They went only about five miles per hour because they were used for sightseeing, not for thrills. But over the years, they got bigger, faster, and more violent—kind of like the stock market.

Well, I'm getting too old to ride these new roller coasters. I need something that doesn't go quite as high and doesn't sink quite as low. That's why I like these funds with low betas. These funds have reduced the ups and downs of this financial 'thrill ride'—giving investors a much more even and stable ride. You still get performance, but you don't get the extreme performance. Are you ready to take some of the jitters out of your investments?"

A Reliable Vehicle

"I just couldn't help but notice the car you were driving. It's a beautiful car and a great choice. Most people buy that car for its reputation of dependability.

Choosing an investment is kind of like choosing a car. There are vehicles built for safety, performance, and reliability. A few years back, everyone wanted high performance vehicles. Although they were really fast, they were not very dependable. Many of them broke down, costing their owners a great deal of money.

Today, people are looking for reliability again—just like your car. They want vehicles with long track records of quality and reliability, rather than ones that are ultra-quick or ultra-safe.

With that in mind, I would like to tell you about an investment that's kind of like your car—it comes with a long track record of reliable performance."

Law of Lift

"If you want to take off in an airplane, do you fly with or against the wind? You fly against it—the contrary wind helps provide lift.

That's the way it is in the markets. If you fly against prevailing popular sentiments, you'll prosper. When everyone is running to low-paying funds, it's probably time to get back in stocks. When everyone is buying growth stocks, it's probably time to buy value stocks. Go against the wind for best results."

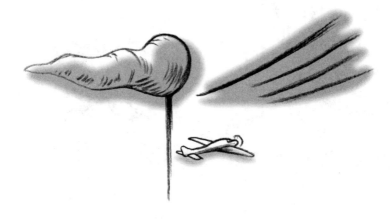

Chasing Losses

"Have you ever seen someone in a casino who had lost a lot of money and was intent on getting back to even? What usually happens? They lose more. This is called chasing losses, and it's what many people do after losing money in a particular investment. They start making foolish decisions in an effort to get back to even. What they need to do is take the loss and put their money in a better place."

Bugs in the Light

"Do you ever notice how certain bugs are drawn to the very thing that will destroy them—the light?

Many investors are this way also. They are drawn to investments that make bright, unheard-of promises. They think they're onto something really special, only to get zapped time after time. All that shimmers is not gold, and if it sounds too good to be true ... "

Money Ball

"Did you happen to read about Billy Beane and the Oakland A's? Over a five-year period, Billy Beane, the GM for the A's, compiled the highest winning percentage in baseball on the lowest payroll!

That's exactly what the managers of this value fund try to do. They look for undervalued talent, buy it cheap, and achieve a high winning percentage year after year."

Hang Ten

"I have spent a lot of time watching surfers, and do you know what they seem to spend most of their time doing? Waiting, not lethargically, but vigilantly. They let a lot of inferior waves go by waiting for the one with the most potential. But, when that good wave comes, they are ready to act quickly."

Coming Up Roses

"When I first started raising roses, I made the mistake of clipping the buds too early—and my rose bushes began to shrink. A more experienced gardener instructed me to wait and allow the bushes to flourish. He told me that when properly cared for, rose bushes grow so hearty and robust that they even get passed down through families.

Our investments are much like the roses. If we clip and harvest too early, our investments may eventually shrink so small that they no longer meet our needs."

Give It Your Best Shot

"When you are playing a best-shot format in golf, the best player typically goes last in order to correct the mistakes of the players that went before.

This is what I share with my golfing clients who want to try some new investment idea. Let's observe first, wait a while, and then give it our best shot."

Waterlogged?

"If you were going on a ten-mile run, you would need to drink about a gallon of water to stay hydrated. You wouldn't drink all the water at the beginning, or it would weigh you down. Instead, you'd space out your drinks as needed.

The same is true with investments. We don't have to make every decision up front—just enough to get started. As we go along, we'll monitor progress and make other decisions at different times in this long run."

Butter or Margarine?

"How many times have you seen science reverse courses? First it is good for you, and then it is bad for you. Years ago, they told us butter was bad and margarine was good. Newspaper and magazine articles pounded the message until we felt guilty about eating butter. Science then comes out and finds that margarine is worse than butter—and then the media runs with that message.

The same idea holds true with investments. One year an investment is bad, and the next year it is the smart thing to do. What—and whom—do you believe? Believe yourself. Figure out what you like and what you are comfortable with, and stop listening to financial magazine headlines that tell you to switch courses every month."

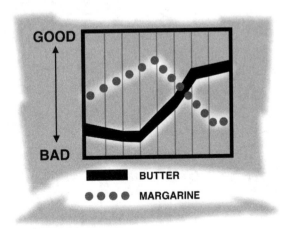

Portage in Rough Waters

"Have you ever taken a canoe trip on a river? If you have, you know that a river has many personalities. You can go along for a while, have smooth sailing in a gentle current, and then go around a bend, suddenly hitting raging rapids. If you do not have the nerve for these rough waters, you will need to steer to the bank and carry your boat.

When it comes time to portage, you want to have a partner or guide who will help you work your way to calmer waters. Better yet, you want a partner or guide who knows this river and helps you get out before you damage your boat on the rocks.

Today we're in rough waters, and it is a good time to portage. Let's get on dry ground and walk until we find waters calm enough to give you the peace of mind you need to get back in the water."

The HALT Rule

"There is a rule of human behavior that many people follow to keep their actions in check when emotions run high—the HALT Rule. The HALT Rule warns people to avoid saying or doing anything when they are:

- **H**ungry to get back money they lost. They become vulnerable.

- **A**ngry over poor advice or returns. They may become overly cautious.

- **L**onely and feeling abandoned by an advisor. They may listen to people whom they ought to ignore.

- **T**ired of the ups and downs. They may lock up their money and surrender flexibility with their assets. The best thing to do is wait until a more rational response arises."

Chasing the Hot Fund

"Have you ever sat in traffic in a lane that's not moving and watched people switch to the empty lane next to you? You become increasingly frustrated and annoyed by your lack of progress and all the people passing you—so you switch lanes. No sooner do you switch lanes then the traffic stops in that lane.

This is exactly what happens to investors who chase this year's hot fund. History shows that those who constantly 'change lanes' to the year's hottest funds don't keep up with next year's overall average returns."

(Contributed by Brett VanBortel)

Stock Value Versus Yield

What do you tell retirees who are receiving monthly income from their investments but are worried about the fluctuations in the value of the investments? One advisor used the following illustration.

"If you owned farmland, would you be more concerned about your yearly yield or fluctuations in the value of your land? Farmers are more concerned about getting paid each year for their crops than they are about land values—which move up and down.

That's the way it is with your investments. Even though some of the underlying investments may move up and down, your number one concern is to make sure you get your check every month."

Other Books by Scott West and Mitch Anthony

- *StorySelling for Financial Advisors*

Other Books by Mitch Anthony

- *The New Retirementality–Planning Your Life and Living Your Dreams ... at any Age You Want*

- *Your Clients for Life–The Definitive Guide to Becoming a Successful Financial Life Planner*

- *Selling with Emotional Intelligence–5 Skills for Building Stronger Client Relationships*

- *Making the Client Connection (co-authored with Gary DeMoss)*

- *The Daily Dose–240 Stories and Ideas that Motivate and Inspire*

Books are available at a special quantity discount rate for use as premiums and sales promotions or for use in corporate training programs.

For ordering information,
contact **Advisor Insights Press** at **(507) 282-2723**
or email **deb@mitchanthony.com.**